As an organisational psychologist and a director at training and development consultancy Talentspace, Rob Yeung PhD helps both organisations and individuals to achieve their goals. He is frequently asked by organisations to interview candidates, design assessment centres and train their interviewers. He writes the questions for interviewers to ask and tells them the answers they should listen out for.

He frequently appears as an expert commentator on television including CNN and BBC news programmes. Rob presents numerous television programmes including the series *How To Get Your Dream Job* for the BBC. As an international speaker, he is in demand to speak on topics such as emotional intelligence, entrepreneurship, leadership, and becoming a high achiever. He is also the author of more than a dozen international bestsellers including *E is for Exceptional: The New Science of Success* (Pan Books) and *How To Win: The Argument, the Pitch, the Job, the Race* (Capstone).

To learn more about Rob's other books or to bring him to your organisation or event, please visit www.robyeung.com.

www.twitter.com/robyeung

www.facebook.com/drrobyeung

Also published by Constable & Robinson

How to Write an Impressive CV
and Cover Letter

How To Pass Psychometric Tests

Psychometric Tests for Graduates

Management Level Psychometric
and Assessment Tests

The Definitive Guide to Passing the
Policing Recruitment Process

Smart Answers to Tricky Interview Questions

Fifth Edition

Dr Rob Yeung

A HOW TO BOOK

ROBINSON

ROBINSON

First published in Great Britain in 2002 by How To Books,
an imprint of Constable & Robinson Ltd.

This edition published in 2015 by Robinson

3 5 7 9 10 8 6 4 2

A CIP catalogue record for this book
is available from the British Library.

ISBN: 978-1-4721-1901-8

Typeset by Mousemat Design Limited
Printed and bound in Great Britain by CPI Group (UK) Ltd, Croydon CR0 4YY

Papers used by Robinson are from well-managed forests and
other responsible sources

MIX
Paper from
responsible sources
FSC
www.fsc.org   FSC® C104740

Robinson
An imprint of
Little, Brown Book Group
Carmelite House
50 Victoria Embankment
London EC4Y 0DZ

An Hachette UK Company
www.hachette.co.uk

www.littlebrown.co.uk

How To Books are published by Robinson, an imprint of Little, Brown Book Group.
We welcome proposals from authors who have first-hand experience of their subjects.
Please set out the aims of your book, its target market and its suggested
contents in an email to Nikki.Read@howtobooks.co.uk

CONTENTS

PREFACE

I make my living from interviewing candidates. Employers ask me to train their interviewers and design assessment centres for them. In writing this book, I'm a gamekeeper turned poacher. So trust me when I say that I know the kinds of questions that interviewers are going to ask.

You want to succeed at interviews. Perhaps you have a suspicion that you aren't putting yourself across to the very best of your ability during interviews. Or maybe you haven't attended an interview in a while and simply want to do some preparation. Whatever your situation, this is the book for you. You know you can do the job – you just need some help in persuading interviewers to give you the chance to prove it.

Well, here's a secret: Succeeding at interviews is like succeeding in a game. Yes, an interview is a game. And, like any other game, interviewing has rules. Sure, some of the rules are unspoken and an interviewer will never tell you to your face that you have broken a rule. But if you break the rules, you will not get offered the job. Follow the rules, and you will get offered the job. It's that simple. Because the person who gets the job is not always the best person for the job; more often than not, they simply know the most about how to get hired.

I wrote the first edition of this book because I was seeing too many candidates who were just not doing themselves justice. With this fifth edition, I've added further questions that interviewers can ask as well as more sample answers to illustrate how to deal with those tough interview topics. I've also added some of my top tips on creating outstanding CVs and covering letters that are sure to get you invited to more interviews.

But I want to stress that getting offered the job isn't just about what you say – it's also about *how* you say it. So even though you must have good answers to the many questions that interviewers may ask you, you also have to think about how you use your voice and body language to help you get your personality and confidence across to wow the interviewers.

To help you get the most from this fifth edition, I've laid out some of the most important advice in the book using the following icons:

 These speech bubbles highlight sample answers that illustrate how to deal with some of the tough interview questions you may be asked. However, remember that to succeed in your own interviews, you must work out your own response rather than simply learning the sample answers off-by-heart!

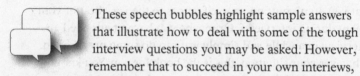 *These ticks point to tips and key ideas that will help you to show yourself off in the best possible light and really impress the interviewers.*

I'm confident that this book covers just about every interview scenario that you might have to deal with. Filled with just about every question that you might be asked as well as examples of proven answers, it will help you prepare responses that are perfect for you. Never be caught out by an interview question ever again. Perhaps you want to join a big international company or a local firm. Maybe you want to work in the private or public sector. Whether you are a school leaver looking for your first job or a senior executive searching for a better job, I guarantee you will learn something new from this book. Whatever you are looking for, you can be confident of making a great impression and acing that interview. So prepare to stand out from the other candidates, and land the job you want. Your next job is within arm's reach!

Chapter 1

DOING YOUR HOMEWORK

In this chapter …
- **Understanding what interviewers are looking for**
- **Learning to decipher job adverts**
- **Researching employers**
- **Making contact by telephone**
- **Getting invited to more interviews**

Anyone can improve their performance at interview. No matter how much you hate interviews, no matter how long it has been since you had an interview, no matter how nervous you might feel, I can guarantee you that doing your homework will boost your confidence and improve your chances of securing a job.

Being invited to an interview is a significant step. Many employers see hundreds of CVs or application forms and only shortlist a handful of candidates to invite to interview. You should pat yourself on the back for getting this far. So don't mess it up now.

There are a few people who are naturally extroverted and able to excel during interviews. But for most people it doesn't come naturally. And that's why success at interviews usually comes down to good preparation and practice. Long before they get in front of any interviewers, the best candidates have spent many hours researching the organisation and the nature of the role, working out answers to likely interview questions, and then rehearsing to make sure they can present themselves as confident, enthusiastic people. In fact, I'd say that as much as 90 percent of what determines success at interview comes down to good preparation and rehearsal.

Candidates who do experience interview nerves get the most out of preparation. Many candidates feel nervous during interviews because they are worried what an interviewer might ask them. But if you have done your preparation, you will be ready to answer any question that an interviewer could ask you. Well-prepared candidates usually find that a large chunk of their anxiety about interviews simply melts away when they feel confident in their preparation.

The more you prepare, the greater your chances will be of coming across as a confident candidate who deserves the job. And this chapter covers exactly what you need to research and prepare before you face any interviewer.

Always write up some notes about each organisation that you have an interview with. You can look at your notes again on the morning of your interview to refresh your memory as to key points.

UNDERSTANDING THE SECRETS OF INTERVIEW SUCCESS

It goes without saying that interviewers want to hire good candidates. But what *exactly* are they looking for? The answer lies in the 'four Cs' of interview characteristics:

■ **Competence** – interviewers want to hire candidates who have the knowledge, skills and qualities to make a difference to their organisations. They are not just looking for any old person to fill the position, but somebody who can learn quickly, go the extra mile, and help the team to achieve its goals. *Successful candidates show interviewers that they have a track record of achieving goals on behalf of their employers.*

- **Commitment** – interviewers want to hire people who will stay in the job for a while. They don't want to hire someone and train them up only for that person to leave after a few months and for them to have to recruit, interview and train another person all over again. *Successful candidates demonstrate their commitment to each different job they interview for.*

- **Confidence** – employers want to hire people who feel comfortable dealing with a range of situations, such as asserting themselves with colleagues and customers. *Successful candidates think about how they use their voice, eye contact and body language to convey that they are poised and self-assured.*

- **Chemistry** – interviewers don't want to hire robots. They want to hire candidates that they feel they get on with – candidates they feel they could share a joke with, have a drink with after work, and so on. *Successful candidates focus as much on building rapport with the interviewers as on answering the questions themselves.*

Bear these key lessons in mind as you read through the rest of the advice in this book.

STUDYING JOB ADVERTS FOR CRUCIAL INFORMATION

Always keep copies of all the job adverts that you have responded to. It can take anywhere from several weeks to a few months before you get invited to interview and you don't want to have to rely on your memory alone to uncover the questions you may be asked.

Begin your homework by returning to the original advert that alerted you to the vacancy. Read through the job advert and take a look at the key words and phrases in the advert to help you to figure out what the key skills and characteristics required for the job are. Then you will be able to prepare for the questions that the interviewer is most likely to ask you.

> *Use a highlighter pen to pick out key phrases in the job advert. And then brainstorm at least three possible questions that an interviewer could ask you about each of those key phrases.*

Consider the following three examples:

Figure 1

EXCITING OPPORTUNITY FOR A PERSONAL ASSISTANT!

Gold Asset Management Limited is looking for a <u>personal assistant</u> to support a busy Managing Director.

You will schedule appointments, <u>deal with travel arrangements</u> for his frequent international trips and use the <u>latest computer software</u> to prepare presentations for him. You will also manage occasional <u>projects in liaison with external clients</u>.

To be successful in this role, you will need to be <u>highly self-motivated</u>. Central London location. £ dependent on experience.

Email: ashley.peterson@gold-assetmanagement.co.uk

So what does the advert in Figure 1 say about the questions that you could be asked? Looking at some of the underlined key words and phrases, we can deduce the following:

■ As the job is looking for a 'personal assistant', you would need to be ready to talk about your previous experience in other roles as a personal assistant. The interviewer might ask: 'What have your previous bosses been like in the past?' 'What kind of person do you most enjoy working with?'

- 'Deal with travel arrangements' suggests that you might need to be able to respond to questions such as: 'Your Managing Director needs to be in Paris on Friday afternoon. It is now Thursday afternoon and the airline has just rung to tell you that they have had to cancel the flights. What would you do now?'

- Be ready to talk about your experience of the 'latest computer software'. What packages are you familiar with?

- The phrase 'projects in liaison with external clients' actually throws up two separate areas to cover. What is your experience of having managed projects? And be ready to talk about examples of how you have dealt with the demands of clients.

- Since the advert is looking for someone who is 'highly self-motivated', would you be able to provide examples of how you have motivated yourself at work?

Here is a second job advert:

Figure 2

IT SALES EXECUTIVE

We are looking to appoint two extra sales executives with experience of selling IT hardware and software.

The successful candidate will have:
- good working <u>knowledge of the ABC and XYZ hardware systems</u>;
- excellent <u>presentation skills</u>;
- a proven <u>track record of selling</u> to clients, either face-to-face, through telesales, or a combination of the two.
- the ability to <u>work independently without supervision</u>.

Please contact Sushma Patel for further details and an application form by calling 020 3458 5681.

Reading the advert in Figure 2, we can deduce that the interviewers may want to discuss topics such as:

- Your knowledge of the ABC and XYZ systems. For example, if you do not have working knowledge of one of those systems, you might need to come up with good examples of how you learnt quickly about other systems. You need to be able to prove to the interviewers that you could get up to speed about their systems without problems.
- Your 'presentation skills'. In order to impress the interviewers, you should be able to talk about how you prepared presentations, perhaps drafted any slides, and then presented them to clients or customers.
- Your 'track record of selling'. You must be able to explain how you managed to sell to customers in the past. How did you overcome their objections? What tactics did you use to understand their needs and close the sale? What size orders did those customers place with you? Interviewers can sometimes ask very detailed questions, so make sure you can talk in depth about the situations you dealt with in the past.
- Your ability to 'work independently without supervision'. Can you think of situations in which you took the initiative and got on with a job rather than simply sitting around waiting for your boss to tell you what to do?

Here's a final example for a managerial job:
Reading the job advert opposite, we can make certain deductions about the key skills that may be involved and therefore the questions they might ask:

- The fact that the company describes itself as working in 'industrial components' and 'manufacturing' immediately throws up two questions that an interviewer might ask. Firstly, 'Do you have any relevant experience in this sector?'

Figure 3

GRADUATE MANAGEMENT OPPORTUNITY

Europe's premier <u>industrial components</u> company Bayern McFadden is seeking a <u>graduate-calibre</u> manager to <u>revitalise</u> its UK <u>manufacturing</u> division.

Successful candidates will have significant experience of <u>leading teams</u> to <u>turn around business performance</u>. You will <u>work alongside continental European managers</u> to <u>deliver results</u>. <u>MBA</u> would be an advantage.

Considerable salary and bonus for the right candidate.

For an application form, please contact Janet Baxendale on 030 7000 8080.

Secondly, if you do not have directly relevant experience, 'Why are you interested in working in this sector?'

■ 'Graduate-calibre' does not mean that you necessarily need to be a graduate. If you managed to get an interview, then obviously you have the right experience. But you may be asked questions about the reasons why you did not go to university and how you have you developed your skills over the years.

■ The words 'revitalise' and 'turn around business performance' indicate that the division is not doing very well. So be ready to answer questions such as: 'In your career so far, can you give me an example of how you have improved the performance of a business?' and 'If we offered you the job, what steps would you first take to tackle the performance of the division?'

■ 'Leading teams' suggests that the interviewer might ask a question such as: 'When working with a new team, how do you go about building your relationships with the team?'

■ The phrase 'work alongside continental European managers' throws up questions about your language skills and previous experience of working across cultural boundaries.

- The phrase 'deliver results' suggests that you are able to set targets, work to deadlines, and achieve measurable benefits.
- Finally, if you do not have an 'MBA', then you must be able to give a credible reason why you should still be considered for the job if you do not possess an MBA or some similar business qualification.

By looking closely at the job advert, you should be able to work out the main topics that the interviewers are likely to want to cover. Chapters 4 to 8 will give you some advice on how to construct good responses.

RESEARCHING YOUR PROSPECTIVE EMPLOYER

Employers like to feel special. They want to hire candidates who want to work for them rather than any other company. And being able to talk about the reasons you want to join this particular organisation is a way of making yourself stand out from most of the crowd.

At a minimum, you should be able to find out answers to the following questions:

- **What sort of business are they in?** What services or products does the organisation offer?
- **What are the company's vision, mission, and values?** In other words, *what* does the organisation aim to achieve and *how* does it aim to do it?
- **Who are the key people within the organisation?** For example, if the chairman, chief executive, or any of the directors are well-known figures in the local or international community, make sure you know their names so that you

don't look confused should an interviewer drop their names into the discussion.

- **What is the organisation's strategy for the future?** What plans or investments do they have lined up going forwards?
- **Approximately how many staff does the organisation employ?** Are they a very large or a very small employer?
- **Where does the organisation have offices?** Is it concentrated in just one location or many locations around the country or even the world?
- **Who are their competitors?** What products and services do those competitors offer? And how do the products and services of your prospective employer differ from those of its competitors?
- **What are the trends across the industry?** What are the main challenges and opportunities facing organisations within this sector?

Be prepared to invest serious effort in researching each prospective employer. Avoid simply memorising facts about the organisation – try to form your own opinions about it too.

Read and read some more

In your preparation, you should read ravenously. Any snippet you pick up could make the difference in showing that you have invested time and effort to understand the organisation.

Be sure to read any marketing literature that the organisation has. For example, if the company sends information out, you should ring the customer care line and ask for brochures and so on. Most organisations have websites too and, quite frankly, candidates who don't read up on an organisation on their website really do not deserve to get offered the job!

Of course, search engines such as Google provide easy access to a large volume of information about employers too. One of the best tactics is simply to enter the organisation's name into the search box at www.google.com and to read all about the company there.

However, some information may only be available in specialist trade publications. So don't assume that you can do all your research from the comfort of your own home. Putting in a couple of hours to visit a university library or city business library may pay dividends when it comes to telling the interviewer about some insight that you have gleaned that other candidates have not spotted.

Look, listen, and learn

Reading up on an organisation is a great start. But top candidates go further by putting in some legwork to research potential employers too. Make sure to:

- Visit physical locations of the employer. For example, go to several different branches of a bank, a retailer's shops on the high street, a car manufacturer's showrooms, and so on. If you can buy, try, or get a feel for the company's products or services before an interview, you will give yourself a significant advantage.
- Talk to people who are associated with the organisation. For example, pop into the company's shops, branches, or showrooms, and talk to the staff. Tell them that you are thinking about taking a job with the company and ask for a few of their thoughts. You never know what information you might pick up. Someone could even warn you about favourite questions that the interviewers at head office like to ask!
- Ask friends, family, and acquaintances for information about

the organisation. Even if they do not know anything about the organisation, you may find that they know people who have had contact with the organisation. Even talking to someone in the same industry could be helpful. So ask the people you know for introductions to people who may know either about the particular organisation or its general industry.

Try to find out something about the organisation that isn't written on its website or in any literature. Interviewers are always much more impressed by candidates who have taken the time to move beyond desk research.

Telephone ahead

Apart from the time, date, and location of the interview, you will also need to know who you are going to be interviewed by. But there is other information that you should find out before your interview as well. Simply pick up the telephone and politely try to ask the recruitment coordinator, a relevant human resources manager, or the interviewer's secretary:

■ How many people will be interviewing you?
■ What are their names and job titles?
■ Will there be just one interview or perhaps a series of interviews, or even some tests and an assessment centre?
■ Do they have a job description for the vacancy? And will they let you see it beforehand?

Also try to sort out practical issues such as getting directions, or asking whether you will be able to claim for travel expenses. You do not want to bother the interviewer about such relatively trivial matters.

Be sure to be unfailingly polite on the telephone. Any rudeness to a receptionist or secretary could easily get reported back to your interviewer.

GETTING INVITED TO MORE INTERVIEWS

If you find that you're not getting offered as many interviews as you'd like, I suggest that you take a good look at both your CV and the covering letters or emails that you've written to go alongside of them.

Most employers receive many dozens (if not hundreds) of applications for every vacancy. So you really need to put in the time to make sure that you stand out from the crowd.

Remember the basics

I almost hate to mention these, because you probably already know them. But I do see candidates making certain mistakes over and over again. So here are some essential pointers for creating great CVs and covering letters:

- Print on good quality A4 white paper. Avoid using coloured paper as employers hate such attention-grabbing tactics.
- Use the same font or typeface on both your CV and covering letter. Use the default font size that comes with your word processing software. Avoid using a smaller font size in an attempt to pack in more information as doing so implies that you can't prioritise what's important and what's not.
- Use the standard margins, headers and footers for your CV. Avoid shrinking these so you can pack more information onto your CV – this also smacks of an inability to summarise your skills concisely.

- Check the spelling of both documents and ideally have a friend check them over too to ensure you haven't missed any mistakes.

In constructing both your CV and covering letter, a great principle is to *include only information that is relevant to the job you're applying for*. For example, if you're applying for a job in computing and have four years' experience of working with computers and three years of having worked in retail, then by all means emphasise your computing experience by writing about your relevant responsibilities and achievements in depth. You'll want to write much less about the years you spent working in retail to avoid giving the impression that you should be working in retail.

Keep your CV to two pages – or three if you have more than 15 years' work experience. Your CV should be a concise summary of your top skills and key achievements, not just a list of everything you've ever done. Keep your covering letter to one page.

Prune your CV

I interview lots of candidates on behalf of employers so I see quite a few CVs. One of the main faults I see on CVs is that they are often too cluttered. Being cluttered isn't *wrong* exactly, but it does mean that an employer finds it more difficult to see what's important.

Here are my top tips for ensuring that your CV makes a great impact:

- **Write mostly about your last three jobs and/or the last 5 to 7 years**. Say you've got more than a decade of work experience. Truth is that what you did ten, 12, 15 (or more) years ago isn't actually that interesting to an employer. An employer wants to focus on what you're currently doing or what you've achieved recently. Skills get outdated and technology moves on so quickly. By all means write a couple of paragraphs about your responsibilities and achievements in your last two or three roles and/or over the last 5 to 7 years. But if you have other jobs from the distant past, you should write just a couple of sentences on each. Certainly, no employer will make a decision whether or not to invite you to interview based on anything you were doing from before the year 1995!

■ **Remove your date of birth and nationality from the CV**. For a few years now, it's been illegal for employers to ask candidates to reveal their date of birth (to prevent discrimination on the basis of age). So take your age and birth date off your CV. You also don't need to include your nationality. An employer will assume that you have the right to work for them anyway.

■ **Take off any mention of your references**. Not all employers ask to check references. And you certainly don't want employers contacting your referees for references without you knowing about it. You don't even need to include a sentence that says 'References on request' as employers will simply ask if they want them.

Tailor your CV

A good principle to bear in mind is that you should *tailor every CV you send off*. Yes, the CV you send to one employer almost certainly needs to be different to the one you send to another employer.

As little as ten years ago, job hunters could get away with having just the one CV to send to every employer. But savvy candidates realise that tailoring their CVs to the needs of different employers gives them a huge advantage.

The traditional CV typically starts with your address and contact details and then follows on with a section about your employment history in reverse chronological order (i.e. most recent job first). Perhaps the easiest way to tailor your CV to each different vacancy is by adding a section headed 'Skills' or 'Skills/Achievements' on your CV (see next page).

Here are a few pointers to creating a new, more dynamic CV that you can tailor to different employers (and get yourself invited to more interviews):

- Shorten the part of your current CV in which you write about your employment history. Aim to reduce it enough so that you free up around a half-page to two-thirds of a page.
- Create a new section with the title 'Skills'. In this section, write down the key skills that the employer believes are important for the job. Take a look back at the section 'Studying job adverts for crucial information' earlier on in this chapter to remind yourself how to do it.
- For each skill, write down a couple of sentences that explain to the interviewer what you did. You need to show the interviewer that you really do possess that skill.
- Finally, think of any achievements that you can include as evidence about your skill. For example, do mention it if you exceeded any targets or received any commendations, awards or even compliments.

 Remember, remember to craft different CVs for different jobs. The clues as to the skills you need to mention on your CV can be found in the job advert for the vacancy.

John Mitchell

Address: 197a Liberty Avenue, London W85 KLP.
Telephone: 050 9031 8234. Mobile: 07011 923 1871.
Email: johnmit1000@email.co.uk

Skills

Results focus. Exceeded my targets last year – sold 3.8 per cent more than my target. I was also within the top 20 per cent of the sales force last year. I do this by being one of the first people into the office every morning as I believe I can achieve so much by getting into work at 8am every day.

Presentation skills. Writing slides and presenting material both internally to colleagues as well as externally to clients. Presenting 3 to 4 times a week, for up to an hour at a time. I always write my presentations by thinking about what the client wants to hear and what will persuade them to work with me. I won new clients Hillman Foods (who generated a six-figure fee for us last year) and Wiltshire Grove Farms (who are likely to generate a six-figure fee for us by the end of this year).

Interpersonal skills. Working internally with both marketing and finance to ensure we offered clients a seamless service. This often involved being assertive, but at the same time knowing when to be flexible in order to get the right result for everybody. For example, I had to put together a business case in order to persuade my boss to let us spend double our usual budget on the pitch to Hillman Foods (which was ultimately successful).

Employment

2012–present. Account Manager at advertising firm HKM Crown Associates. I was first point of contact for clients including Hillman Foods, Goji Products, Tudor Lodge, and Wiltshire Grove Farms.
2009–2012. Account Executive at marketing agency The Ideas Company. Worked closely with clients on campaigns.
2007–2009. Sales person at retailer Sensations. Selling products directly to customers at one of the flagship stores on Oxford Street in London.

Education/qualifications

B.Sc. physical sciences, University of Manchester (2003)
Diploma in marketing strategy, Central Guildhall College (2008)

Tailoring your first CV will take a little bit of time. But tailoring the second will take less time and each one after that will get easier and easier. And you can rest assured that you are making your CV so much more noteworthy and interesting to employers.

Write covering letters that show what you can contribute

To further boost your chances of being picked to attend an interview, make sure you're writing great covering letters too. Again, you need to tailor your covering letter to the needs of each individual employer. It's no good simply sending more or less identical covering letters. The kind of achievements that make one employer take notice of you may not be of any interest to another employer.

Again, take a careful look at the job advert. Pick out the two or three key skills or qualities that the advert seems to be asking for. And make sure you write about them.

Here's an idea of what a covering letter should include:

Your address and telephone number

Name, job title and address of the person you're writing to

Today's date

Dear *their name*,

A single sentence telling the employer which job you're applying for, and where you read about it. Then another sentence saying that you're enclosing your CV.

A short paragraph highlighting the skill, quality or achievement of yours that you think will most excite and interest the employer.

A short paragraph highlighting a second skill, quality or achievement of yours that will interest the employer.

Possibly, a third paragraph talking about a third relevant skill, quality or achievement.

Finally, a sentence expressing your enthusiasm/excitement/interest in the job.

Yours sincerely/faithfully,

Your signature

John Mitchell,
197a Liberty Avenue,
London W85 KLP.

Mrs Jeanette Kahn,
Human Resources Coordinator,
Uplift Advertising,
The Millhouse Tower,
192 Burbank Street,
London EC3 95J.

5th January 2015

Dear Mrs Kahn,

I read with great interest the advertisement in *Advertising and Marketing Week* for an Account Director to join the team at Uplift Advertising. I attach my CV and would like to highlight my continuing career progression and success at delivering results in advertising.

In my career as an Account Manager at top advertising firm HKM Crown Associates, I have a track record of focusing on results. Rather than waiting passively for clients to approach us, I am constantly networking and trying to build relationships with potential clients. For example, I have breakfast meetings with potential clients on 2 or 3 days every week and attend a similar number of evening events too, networking in both formal and informal situations, for example with local chambers of commerce, business associations, and at conferences. As such, I was solely responsible for approaching the managing director and marketing director at Goji Products and turning this into a significant piece of business for us.

Your advert says that you are looking for people with strong presentation skills and I possess these in abundance. I prepare my pitches assiduously and get all of the members of my team to rehearse together so that we are well-prepared and confident. The marketing director at our client Tudor Lodge said in an email that I was "inspirational" and "the single biggest factor" in winning them over during the pitch presentation that ultimately brought in the client.

I'm genuinely excited by the opportunity and look forward to hearing from you soon.

Yours sincerely,

John Mitchell
John Mitchell

Opposite is an example of what a covering letter might look like for John Mitchell:

Notice that the covering letter works together with the CV. So our candidate John Mitchell read the employer's advert and chose to focus on 'results focus' on the CV and 'a track record of focusing on results' in the covering letter. He also mentions 'presentation skills' in both the covering letter and CV.

Mention at least two relevant skills or achievements in your covering letter. Remember that these should be the skills or achievements that are most relevant to the particular employer.

Again, this approach will take a little longer than simply sending the same covering letter out to multiple employers. But you help yourself to boost significantly your chances of actually getting invited to interview.

IN SUMMARY ...

- Bear in mind that employers are not only looking for skills and know-how (i.e. competence) but also confidence, commitment and interpersonal chemistry.
- Read and re-read the job advert to establish likely topics that may crop up during the interview and possible questions you may be asked.
- Research the organisation that you are going to be interviewed by. Employers always warm to candidates who can demonstrate they have taken the time to find out about the organisation.
- Sort out the logistics of the interview well before you have to turn up for the interview.
- If you're finding that you're not getting invited to as many interviews as you'd like, be sure to review your CVs and covering letters from the point of view of the companies you'd like to work for.

Chapter 2

MAKING A STRONG IMPACT

In this chapter ...
■ **Dressing appropriately for interviews**
■ **Building rapport and focusing on interpersonal chemistry**
■ **Listening and responding carefully to questions**
■ **Providing powerful examples to demonstrate your competence**
■ **Keeping it short and sweet**

Interviewers make up their minds based on many factors – only one of which is what candidates say. Just as important as *what* you say is *how* you say it. For example, a candidate who says 'I'm really keen to work here' while shaking visibly, mumbling the words in a barely audible and flat tone, and avoiding eye contact will create a rather poor impression. A candidate who says exactly the same words – 'I'm really keen to work here' – while smiling appropriately, speaking clearly in an enthusiastic way, and making strong eye contact creates a much stronger impact.

How you come across in your appearance and manner is of particular importance within the first few minutes of the interview. You're probably heard some interviewers say that they make up their minds about candidates in the first few minutes of meeting them. How you look and behave in those first few minutes can make a critical difference between success and failure.

This chapter focuses on making not only a great first

impression, but also managing your impact throughout the entire interview.

 Remember that chemistry *makes up a huge part of an interviewer's decision as to which candidate to hire.*

DRESSING FOR SUCCESS

It's human nature to judge others based on what they look like. We all do it when we see someone with purple hair and a nose ring, someone wearing expensive designer labels, or another person with overly tight trousers and a low-cut top. We assume characteristics about other people based purely on what they look like. So why should it be any different for interviewers when they meet you for the first time too?

If you wear clothes that look like they are appropriate only for lounging around at home, the interviewer may decide on your behalf that you would be better off at home rather than working for their organisation. If you look dishevelled, they may assume that your mind is also a bit dishevelled and that you may not be very good at organising your work activity.

Of course interviewers are rarely likely to tell you that they don't like what you wear. But that doesn't stop them from thinking on it, and deciding to choose another more appropriately dressed candidate instead. So think carefully about what you are going to wear and ensure you always create a great first impression.

 Bear in mind that interviewers (often subconsciously) believe that your appearance is the outward manifestation of your personality. What does your appearance say about your *personality?*

Dress appropriately for your industry

It used to be so much easier in the 'old days' when everyone would wear a smart suit for interviews. However, wearing a suit to the wrong organisation could mark you out as boring and precisely the wrong kind of person to be working for them. For example, creative industries such as advertising agencies often pride themselves on being hotbeds of trendy ideas and may look down on candidates who are suited and booted.

The best way to figure out what to wear is to do some research as follows:

- Visit the office of your chosen employer and stand outside. Watch the flow of people in and out and take note of what they are wearing. However, be careful as managers who know that they need to see clients or interview candidates may dress more smartly than they would do normally.
- Call the organisation and ask about the dress code. Do not allow yourself to be fobbed off by a receptionist. Ask politely to speak to the secretary or personal assistant of the manager who will be interviewing you. Explain that you wanted to check the dress code so you do not stand out for all the wrong reasons.

If you are planning to dress down, make sure you are 100 percent certain that this is the right move – only if you have been told personally by the interviewer's assistant that he or she will be dressed casually. If you are in any doubt as to what to wear, err on the side of caution and abide by the following guidelines for men and women.

Be very careful of dressing down. As a rule of thumb, it's better to be overdressed than underdressed. A man, for example, could simply remove his tie and unbutton his top button to appear more relaxed – while women's suits tend to be suitable both in formal as well as smart-casual situations.

Understand the rules for men

The rules for men are fairly simple:

- Wear a dark wool suit. Navy blue and grey are the most acceptable colours. Suits that are 100 percent wool are the best as they are naturally much more crease resistant than even fabrics that have been specially treated to resist creases. If you can't afford 100 percent wool, at least buy a wool blend rather than entirely man-made fabrics as they can often look cheap and may quickly look shiny after only a handful of outings. Make sure that the suit is smart, clean, and well fitted. If it has been a while since you last wore your suit, make sure that it still fits you and does not need dry-cleaning.

- Wear a long-sleeved shirt, either in white or a pale colour such as cream or light blue. While polyester or poly/cotton mixes may be more crease-resistant, they also tend to 'breathe' less than 100 percent cotton shirts, which can be problematic if you have a tendency to sweat much. Damp patches are deeply, deeply unattractive.

- Choose an uncomplicated 100 percent silk tie. Given that you can buy plain silk ties from many high street chains for around £10, there really is no excuse not to. And don't obsess too much about the colour. Simply choose a single-colour tie or one with a very straightforward pattern. I've read some so-called experts saying that certain colours send out signals to the interviewers about your personality, but please ignore them. Allow your words to speak louder than your fashion sense.

- Wear plain black or navy socks. Avoid wearing novelty socks at all costs – again, you want your words to speak more loudly than your socks. And leave the white or other coloured socks for the gym or football pitch.
- Wear black shoes. Italians can get away with brown – but it just does not seem to work for the British!
- Wear (at most) three items of jewellery – a watch, a wedding band, and perhaps cuff links with a double-cuff shirt. Nothing more. Even a tie clip looks dated in the 21st century.

Invest at least a week of your wages or salary when buying a new suit. What you wear is an essential investment in your career.

Understand the rules for women

The rules for women are much more complex as women's fashions do change from year to year. The fashion industry will dictate that a certain colour is in fashion this year and a different one the next year. However, stick to the following guidelines:

- Wear a two-piece suit as opposed to separates. And bear in mind that the business world often lags the fashion world by several years – so err on the side of choosing a suit that is more traditional and conservative than what the fashion magazines may be telling you to buy.
- Spend as much as you can afford on a good quality suit. Choose a fabric that does not wrinkle easily – avoid linen! Women interviewers are often much more critical of female candidates' fashion choices than those of male candidates.
- Wear a jacket and skirt as opposed to jacket and trousers.

Unfortunately, some (typically older, male) interviewers can still be a bit sexist about skirts versus trousers.

- Choose a plain blouse. Don't try to look sexy – as your definition of sexy may unfortunately be an interviewer's definition of tarty.
- Choose matching coloured accessories such as shoes, belts and handbags. And wear shoes that your grandmother would be happy with. Manolo Blahnik's may be the height of fashion – but again some (typically older, male) interviewers in more staid industries may see them as over-the-top.
- Evaluate your overall appearance including your hair and make-up to ensure you project an aura of total professionalism.

Avoid unusual jewellery such as more than one earring per ear or thumb rings. Again you may get a negative reaction from older interviewers and those with more traditional personal values.

You may want to disagree with these guidelines. But I'm only reporting them – I didn't invent them so please don't shoot the messenger! At the end of the day, you can wear what you like, but just be aware that there are some interviewers with quite traditional ideas about what is appropriate or not.

Avoid blunders

Over the years, I have observed that some interviewers can attach a disproportionate amount of meaning to some relatively minor sartorial errors. So make sure that you:

- Polish your shoes. It is a cliché, but some interviewers can get a bit preoccupied when a candidate ruins a good suit by teaming it with scuffed shoes.

- Get a haircut (and/or get your roots done if you dye your hair) a week before the interview. End of discussion.
- Check your personal hygiene – that means your breath and body odour. Ask your best friend in the world for an honest opinion. As an interviewer, I am frequently amazed by candidates who, for example, leave a trail of body odour in their wake or do not realise that they have bad breath. Try this test right now: lick the back of your hand and wait for it to dry then sniff it. *That's* what your breath smells like, so get breath mints to suck on while you wait in reception. Be careful not to wear too much perfume or after-shave too.

A book can't tell you exactly what to wear for every single interview. However, your friends might be able to give you some valuable advice on what to wear. So go ask your friends, colleagues, and partner for their honest opinion. But if you ask them for advice, then be gracious enough to thank them for their advice and, above all, listen to their advice and incorporate some changes into your wardrobe.

Pack a smart bag

You do not have to have a formal briefcase. However, it would help if you have a smart bag or case of some sort to carry with you items such as:

- **Several copies of your CV or application form**. Occasionally, an interviewer may have been drafted in at the last minute and may not have your CV to hand. Handing over a copy when your interviewer doesn't have one will demonstrate your efficiency and professionalism.
- **Samples of any relevant work**. For example, if you are an architect or designer, you may want to bring along plans or diagrams to show the interviewer.

However, do *not* take a notepad and pen along with you. Interview etiquette dictates that the interviewer is the one who is allowed to take notes on you. Taking notes on what the interviewer says (even if you are asking some questions) implies that you have such a poor memory that you can't remember a few simple facts. If you must bring along a notepad and pen, use them only *after* the interview to write up your notes and not during the interview.

Be sure to switch your mobile phone onto silent mode or turn it off entirely. A ringing phone halfway through an interview will not *impress an interviewer.*

BUILDING RAPPORT WITH INTERVIEWERS

Interpersonal chemistry is incredibly important during interviews. Given the choice, many interviewers would rather choose to hire a candidate who may not have all of the right skills but they like rather than one who has the right skills but they don't like.

After all, would you want to work with someone who was technically very good at the job, but rather boring or a bit arrogant? You need to make the interviewer not only think highly of your skills but also *want* to work with you. Skills and experience sometimes don't matter if you don't come across as someone that people could *enjoy* spending time with.

Don't underestimate the power of a smile. Smiles (like yawns) are infectious. Surely it can't be a bad thing to infect your interviewer with a smile and put them in a good mood?

Present your best self

Some so-called experts advise candidates that they should 'be themselves' so that they don't end up being offered the wrong sort of job. But wouldn't you rather be offered the 'wrong' sort of job rather than be offered none at all? You can always turn down jobs that don't suit! And what does 'being yourself' mean anyway?

I bet you don't behave in the same way in front of your parents as you do in front of your boss. I would put money on the fact that you present a different side of your personality to your friends on a lads' or girls' night out than you do to a customer. And there are probably behaviours that you would do at home when you are 'being yourself' such as putting your feet up on the coffee table, drinking straight from the carton, or even burping that you would never do in front of colleagues. So think about an interview as an opportunity to present yourself in the best possible light – use your body language, posture, tone of voice, hand gestures, smiles, and every technique at your disposal to make yourself appear as the kind of professional, committed, enthusiastic person that the interviewers will want to hire.

Focus on first contact

First impressions count. So it makes sense to choreograph the first few minutes of an interview to make sure you deliver a devastatingly professional, confident, and personable first impression. When meeting your interviewer for the first time, be sure to:

- ■ **Arrive early**. Calculate your journey time days before your interview and make sure you can get there on time. If in doubt, get there early and find a local coffee shop where you can relax and get into the right frame of mind. Arrive late and you immediately plant a question in the interviewer's mind: Will this candidate *frequently* arrive late for work?

- **Switch all of your mobile devices off**. Having a mobile phone, pager or BlackBerry making itself heard during an interview isn't going to impress an interviewer. But even allowing a device to vibrate silently isn't a good idea as it will distract you from what you need to be focusing on. So turn them off entirely.

- **Pre-plan some small talk**. Arrive at reception ten or 15 minutes early so you can look around the building for features you could comment on and genuinely praise. For example, look for plaques on the wall commemorating prizes the organisation has won or books filled with press cuttings about the organisation. Look also for original pieces of art, the design of the reception area or building, the landscaped gardens outside, and so on.

- **Follow the interviewer's lead with respect to polite conversation** or 'chit chat'. When the interviewer arrives, being able to talk positively about one or two aspects of their organisation will help to create the impression that you are a friendly, likeable person. But follow the interviewer's lead – while certain interviewers genuinely enjoy making small talk, others may want to press on almost immediately with interview questions.

- **Make eye contact and smile broadly** on first meeting the interviewer. Babies learn to recognise smiles from the age of several weeks; human beings are genetically programmed to warm to others who smile. Even if you feel nervous and don't feel like smiling, force yourself to do so.

- **Shake hands firmly** – but without crushing your interviewer's hand. If you have a tendency to get nervous and for your hands to sweat, hold your hands under a cold tap for a few minutes in the lavatory. Failing that, discreetly keep your right hand wrapped around a handkerchief in your pocket or handbag until you see an interviewer approaching to shake your hand.

- ■ **Wait to be invited to take a seat**. And, as a mark of respect, ask for permission from the interviewer to take off your jacket (particularly from older interviewers who appreciate such nuances of business etiquette).

Sometimes an interviewer may hand you a business card with his or her details on it. If your interviewer does this, be sure to accept the card, thank the interviewer for it and spend a couple of seconds reading it. Make sure you take note of the person's name and job title. Then be sure to put the business card in a conspicuously safe place such as in your wallet, a folio or a top pocket. Avoid simply jamming it in a trouser pocket as an interviewer may take this as a sign of disrespect.

Use your body language and tone of voice throughout the interview

Rapport is not established at any particular point in the interview. Working on building rapport is something that you need to do throughout the interview.

Follow these tips to create a strong and positive impression through your body language:

- ■ **Maintain eye contact** throughout the interview. Research tells us that you should look your interviewer in the eye when they are speaking. It is acceptable to glance away occasionally when it is your turn to speak – for example, many people look at some spot in the middle distance when pausing for a moment to construct an appropriate response to an interview question.

- **Nod** to show that you are paying attention to what the interviewer is saying.
- **'Flash' your eyes** by raising your eyebrows occasionally – again, this shows that you are actively paying attention to what is being said.
- **Smile** and, if appropriate, even show that you have a sense of humour.
- **Use hand movements to emphasise key points.** Watch any good public speaker and you will notice that they use their hands to punctuate their words. For example, many people turn their palms up to indicate sincerity or move their hands slightly more vigorously when they get excited.

Use short utterances such as 'uh-huh' and 'mmm' occasionally to show that you understand and agree with what the interviewer is saying and asking you.

Vocal qualities such as the tone, volume, and inflection of your speech can also have a major effect in projecting your personality and positive characteristics such as enthusiasm and confidence too. Try to:

- **Think about the volume of your speech.** Have you ever been told that you speak a bit too quietly or loudly? Being barely audible could make you sound quite nervous; being too loud could make you appear arrogant.
- **Avoid sounding monotonous.** One of the commonest complaints interviewers make about candidates is that they have flat, lifeless, boring speaking voices. Try to introduce inflection into your words – raise your tone slightly when talking about topics that should excite you (such as why you want the job and when talking about your own achievements) and lower the register of your voice when talking about more

serious topics (such as any regrets or difficult situations you have coped with).

■ **Think about the speed with which you speak**. Speaking too quickly could make you appear nervous; speaking too slowly will drain the energy from your interviewers. Try to vary your speed occasionally. Again, quickening your pace may be appropriate to convey enthusiasm. Slowing down may be useful when you want to appear more thoughtful, considered, and mature.

If the idea of using body language and your tone of voice to build rapport seems baffling, a good exercise is to look around you at the people you work with. The next time you are in a meeting with colleagues or simply having a drink with friends, watch the people around you and ask yourself who looks bored? Who looks motivated and fired up? And then analyse what it is that they say, how they say it, and how their faces, hands and bodies move to give off a good or bad impression. Try to incorporate what they say and do in order to create the right impact during your interviews.

If you're not sure whether you are making best use of your body language and tone of voice, ask a friend to conduct a mock interview with you and give you honest feedback on how you come across.

Minimise any distracting body language

Learn to monitor the unconscious signals that your body sends out during interviews. Many interviewers comment that they get distracted by minor tics or traits of candidates. Typical lapses to look out for include:

- Fidgeting with your hands or playing with a pen, ring, cuff links, curl of hair, etc.
- Tensing up your shoulders.
- Speaking too quickly. If you feel yourself becoming nervous, try swallowing between sentences – this forces you to slow down.
- Biting or chewing your lips.
- Crossing and uncrossing your legs frequently.
- Making wild gestures with your hands (particularly if your interviewer is practically motionless).

If you are worried about your body language, ask your colleagues or close friends whether you have any particular mannerisms when you are nervous.

Start to observe the body language of the people you work with. Notice how their body language often communicates their true feelings and learn from what you see to make sure you communicate only enthusiasm and confidence during your interviews.

LISTENING AND RESPONDING TO THE QUESTIONS THAT ARE ASKED

Interviewers sometimes complain about candidates who answer the question they *think* was asked and not the one that was *actually* asked. For example, a candidate may hear a question

about 'achievements' and proceed to rattle off an answer about
their key strengths, not having heard the interviewer ask a
question that actually enquired about achievements from a
particular period or perhaps from outside of work.

The situation is not helped by the fact that unskilled
interviewers can sometimes inadvertently – or sometimes
deliberately – ask questions that are lengthy, convoluted, and
difficult to answer. In order to make sure that you do not fall
foul of this trap, be sure to:

- Listen to the entire question that is being asked rather than
  just plucking out the key words or trying to predict the
  question that you think the interviewer may ask.
- Take a few moments to think through your answer. If the
  interviewer has asked you a tough question that is an unusual
  variation on what you were expecting, do say 'That's not
  something I've thought about before – could I have a few
  seconds to think about that?' Then allow yourself as long as
  you need to answer the question.
- Don't ignore parts of a question that you may not want to
  answer. For example, when interviewers ask candidates, 'What
  are your strengths and weaknesses?' it irritates them no end
  when candidates talk about their strengths but try to get away
  without revealing any weaknesses.

*Always ask for clarification if you are not 100 percent
sure of the question. 'Sorry, I'm not sure I understand,
could you repeat the question, please?'*

ANSWERING QUESTIONS CONCISELY

Interviewers try their best to listen to candidates. But remember that an interview should be a dialogue rather than a series of lengthy monologues on your part. Bear in mind that an interviewer may have already met several other candidates – the last thing you want to do is talk for so long that you bore your interviewer.

So when an interviewer asks you a simple question, keep your answers short to begin with. Think of each interview answer as the tip of an iceberg. You should aim to answer with a response that lasts for only 20 to 30 seconds. But beneath that surface, you have much more detail to share *if* the interviewer is interested in hearing it.

> *Check that you are providing your interviewer with useful information by asking questions such as 'shall I go on?' 'is this what you were looking for?' or 'would you like an example of that?' rather than droning on at the interviewer.*

PROVIDING EXAMPLES TO ENHANCE YOUR CREDIBILITY

Suppose that an interviewer says to a candidate: 'Tell me about yourself'. Perhaps the candidate responds by saying 'I'm an ambitious person with good managerial skills and a track record of delivering results'. Well, those are just words though, aren't they? Even a candidate who is a lazy person with poor managerial skills and a track record of failing all the time could *claim* to be ambitious and so on.

As such, the difference between a strong candidate and a

weak one often lies in the examples they provide to *prove* their competence. So a strong candidate might go on to say: 'I'm ambitious because I did a course last year in IT skills. I have good managerial skills because I was the only manager last year to be given the top amount of bonus, which is something that my boss would be able to testify to. And I have a track record of delivering results, such as handling a big project for a customer that made our company £80,000 last year.' Immediately, providing examples makes a candidate sound more credible.

Rather than simply make assertions about yourself such as saying 'I believe I'm confident, talented, and hard-working', always provide examples to back up your claims.

Remember that examples paint a much more vivid picture in the mind of the interviewer than do generalised statements that you may make about yourself.

Understand that not all interviewers are skilled interviewers

A skilled interviewer will ask probing questions about problems and opportunities you have faced, and may want examples along with detail as to what you did, why you did it, and what you learned. However, not all interviewers are skilled interviewers. Sometimes, you may be faced with an unskilled interviewer who is more nervous about having to interview a candidate than you are to be interviewed. For example, it's not uncommon for people to get drafted into conducting an interview to cover for a colleague who has been unexpectedly delayed with a customer meeting or due to unforeseen illness!

It is impossible to predict what sort of interviewer you will be faced with. You might think that more senior managers or interviewers in the larger, multinational or more sophisticated companies might be better trained than more junior managers or those in smaller organisations. But that is often not the case.

Consider the following exchange between an unskilled interviewer (I) and a candidate (C):

I: 'Are you a good team player?'
C: 'Yes, I think I am.'
I: 'Thank you. And now the next question …'

As you can see, the interviewer asked a closed-question that could legitimately be answered by a 'yes' or 'no' response. And because the interviewer did not ask for an example, the candidate lost the chance to demonstrate their competence.

However, compare it to an exchange in which the candidate gives a short example – even though the interviewer did not actually ask for one:

I: 'Are you a good team player?'
C: 'Yes, I think I am. I have been taking part in a continuous improvement team for the last six months in addition to my day-to-day responsibilities. I have learnt a lot about working closely in a team to improve how we operate in the business. I can tell you much more about it if you like.'
I: 'There's no need for now, but thank you. And now the next question …'

As you can see, giving an example makes the candidate's response much more vivid – the candidate seems more believable in professing to have good team skills. A skilled interviewer will automatically ask for examples, but an unskilled interviewer may forget to do so. So *try to give short, concrete examples to substantiate your claims and make yourself more memorable.*

PREPARING RELEVANT ANSWERS

What follows in chapters 4 through to 8 are examples of the many questions that you could get asked by interviewers. These hundred or so questions should cover almost anything that an interviewer could throw at you.

However, in reading the questions, the advice, and the sample answers, be sure to think about your own experiences. *Work out the answer to each question that is relevant for you.* You will almost certainly fail if you simply try to learn the sample answers parrot-fashion.

I would strongly recommend that you work through the questions in chapters 4 to 8 and actually write some notes down on how you would answer the questions. Believing that you know what you would say is different from writing it down and then reading it out aloud to hear how it sounds. Putting in the extra effort to prepare your examples and stories will pay considerable dividends when it comes to facing an actual interviewer.

Work out your own answers as you need to find examples that you feel comfortable with – and it is much easier to sound convincing and to project your confidence if you are speaking from personal experience.

Telling the truth

The advice and sample answers in this book lay out what you should ideally be able to say to interviewers. However, your circumstances may dictate that you are unable to give that answer without either exaggerating the truth a bit or telling an outright lie.

It's not my role to sit in judgement and to say that you should never lie and that you must always tell the truth. I know for a fact that quite a few candidates do embellish their experiences, or tell little white lies as well as great big falsehoods. And the truth of the matter is that many candidates get away with it. However, just because *many* candidates get away with it does not mean that *you* will necessarily get away with it.

Remember that many employers check up on references. So be very careful about falsifying details such as your salary, attendance record or other 'hard' facts that an employer could verify by calling your last boss. Some organisations may ask to see your exam certificates too.

To lie or not to lie – that is the question. The ultimate choice is yours.

Weigh up the consequences of being found out to be a liar versus being truthful and hoping that your strengths will compensate for whatever weaknesses or faults you are thinking about covering up.

IN SUMMARY ...

■ Dress conservatively and take advice from trusted friends on how you look.

■ Remember to work on your interpersonal chemistry with interviewers by using your body language and tone of voice to project confidence and enthusiasm.

■ Listen carefully and check that you understand all of the parts of a question before plunging into an answer.

■ Provide short, concrete examples of how you have demonstrated different skills in order to create a vivid picture of your competence for the interviewer.

■ Answer questions briefly and check that the interviewer wants you to go on.

■ Ensure your responses are based on your own experience and not learnt by heart from any book – and think carefully before exaggerating or lying about what you have achieved in your career so far.

Chapter 3

HANDLING NERVES AND BUILDING CONFIDENCE

In this chapter ...
- **Understanding how your beliefs affect your behaviour**
- **Replacing negative thoughts with positive ones**
- **Learning to breathe out tension**
- **Visualising interview success**
- **Appreciating the value of practice, practice, and yet more practice**

Many people find interviews a somewhat scary situation. So you're not alone if you feel a bit nervous about having to attend them. Perhaps you get a dry mouth, racing pulse and sweaty palms. But the good news is that there are practical tips that will help you to manage your nerves and show yourself off in the best possible light. Even better, a modicum of tension can even keep you alert and help you to think more quickly on your feet.

CONNECTING YOUR BRAIN, BODY, AND BEHAVIOUR

Your brain, body, and behaviour are inextricably linked. Change any one of the three – the beliefs you hold in your head, your bodily state, or your behaviour – and you can affect the other two.

For example, scientists have discovered that just thinking negative thoughts can cause your body to release stress chemicals into your bloodstream, which then makes you feel tense. Conversely, thinking positive thoughts can force your heart rate to slow down and help you to feel more relaxed.

Changing your behaviour can also affect your brain and how your body responds to stress. For example, listening to downbeat music can cause your mood to swing downwards; listening to upbeat music forces our brains to switch into a more positive mood.

The tips within this section recognise that your brain (or the beliefs you have about yourself), your bodily state, and your behaviour are linked. Using all of these techniques together will help you to calm your nerves and project a more confident you.

HARNESSING THE POWER OF POSITIVE THINKING

We all have a little voice that goes off in our heads. When things go wrong, our inner critic tells us stuff like how stupid we are, how embarrassing a situation is, how we should avoid similar situations in the future, and so on.

These *automatic negative thoughts* (ANTs) pop unbidden into our heads and can cause us to feel more nervous and behave in ways that aren't helpful. In order to stop these ANTs from crawling into our subconscious, we need to recognise and challenge them.

The key to stamping out your ANTs is to question them when they arise. Try to:

■ **Acknowledge your negative thoughts**. Take a sheet of paper and write down the negative beliefs you have about yourself in the context of interviews and finding a new job.

- **Consciously replace your negative thoughts with positive ones**. Choose some positive phrases about yourself that you can repeat to yourself when you hear your inner critic putting you down. For example, if you hear yourself thinking, 'I'm no good at interviews', perhaps choose instead to say: 'I can be good at interviews if I do my research and preparation'. Or if you find yourself thinking 'I always get so nervous', decide instead to repeat to yourself: 'I will be more confident in this interview than any other interview I've ever been in'.

- **Repeat your positive thoughts over and over to yourself**. When you hear your inner critic speaking up, choose instead to repeat your positive statements instead. You may at first feel a bit silly and your inner critic may start to whisper 'this isn't going to work', but it *will* work. The more frequently you repeat your positive statements about yourself, the more completely you will suppress your inner critic.

Phrase your affirmations positively in terms of what you want to achieve (e.g. 'I am prepared and confident') rather than in terms of what you're trying to avoid (e.g. 'I am not nervous').

LEARNING TO BREATHE RIGHT

Remember that your brain, body, and behaviour are all interconnected. So it stands to reason that if you change what your body is doing, you can also change the feelings that your brain experiences as well as the behaviour you will exhibit during an interview. For example, people who feel nervous often start to breathe more quickly, which can make them feel dizzy and even trigger a panic attack. Conversely, breathing more slowly and deeply can summon up feelings of intense relaxation.

Diaphragmatic breathing is a powerful technique for dispelling tension. First, you have to practise the technique so that you can use it in the moments before an interview. Follow these simple steps:

- Lie on a flat but comfortable surface and place your right hand on your chest and your left hand on your stomach.
- Take slow deep breaths into your stomach. Only your left hand should rise and fall. Practise inhaling to a count of four, holding your breath for a few counts, and then exhaling to a count of four. If you do this for several minutes, you may find that you start to feel very warm, your fingers start to tingle as your body relaxes and pumps blood around your body, and you may feel very relaxed and even slightly sleepy.
- Avoid breathing into the chest area of your lungs. Your right hand should remain motionless. If your right hand is rising and falling, you need to focus on moving your breathing further down into your gut. Breathing into your chest simulates what may happen if you feel angry or nervous.
- Keep practising the technique of diaphragmatic breathing daily until you can reach that relaxed state very quickly. Then practise the technique while sitting upright. Once you have mastered the technique when sitting upright, you are ready to use the technique just prior to an interview – perhaps when you are sitting in reception – to call forth that deep feeling of relaxation.

Use diaphragmatic breathing to relax at any time – for example if you feel nervous the night before an interview and have trouble falling asleep too.

USING MENTAL VISUALISATION

Top sportspeople from golfers and tennis players to Formula 1 drivers all recognise that visualisation can be a powerful technique for helping to create successful outcomes. Amazingly, scientists have found that people who are asked to visualise exercising a muscle can actually build up strength in that muscle without ever stepping into a gym.

Again, this stems from the link between your brain, your body, and your behaviour. If you can think about how a successful interview will look and feel like, you are much more likely to be able to behave in that fashion during an actual interview.

Practise visualising success in a quiet place. Close your eyes and picture yourself getting dressed in your favourite interview outfit. Imagine yourself walking confidently into a reception area. It doesn't matter if you have never seen the building you are going to be interviewed in – the important bit is in visualising yourself succeeding, not the specifics of the building or the room you will be interviewed in. See in your mind's eye how confidently you shake hands, smile, and make polite conversation with the interviewer. And see yourself answering the interviewer's questions in a positive and enthusiastic manner.

Paint as vivid a picture in your mind as you can. If you can make the scene vivid enough, you will be able to trick your body into thinking that it is reality. You can literally think your body into releasing calming endorphins into your bloodstream. The more times you can visualise what success looks like, the more likely you will be to behave in that confident fashion when it comes to actual interviews.

> *Practise mental visualisation every day to get the benefits from it. Don't leave your visualisation exercises until the day before an interview!*

If confidence remains a challenge for you, I've written another book with lots of further tips and techniques for calming frayed nerves and boosting your confidence. Take a look at *Confidence: The Power to Take Control and Live the Life You Want* (Prentice Hall Life).

PRACTISING, REHEARSING AND GETTING IT RIGHT

The very best candidates do not simply think through the questions they might be asked and visualise them. No, the very best candidates practise speaking their answers out loud.

Actors preparing for a big performance on stage do not simply sit quietly and read through their lines. Of course not. They rehearse and practise out loud. They try to speak their lines in the same tone of voice and use the same body movements that they expect to use in front of a live audience. And the same goes for successful interview candidates. The best candidates say their interview responses out loud using a confident tone of voice while using their posture, facial expressions and body language as if they were speaking to a real live interviewer.

The only difference is that you should practise talking about themes rather than learning your lines off by heart and repeating them verbatim every time. You never know precisely what question an interviewer might ask you. So rather than get too wedded to a particular way of answering a question, think about practising out loud the key points you want to get across.

There are several ways you could practise, for example:

- **Practise in front of a mirror**. Flick to a random question in the index at the end of this book and read the question out loud as if an interviewer has asked you it. Then respond out loud. Watch yourself in the mirror and try to observe whether your body language is appropriate too.
- **Record your performance using a video camera**, a webcam, or maybe your smartphone. Watch yourself or at least listen to your voice and be critical about your performance. Listen out for 'ums' and 'ers' or other pauses and stutters and try to eliminate them. Observe your body language and consider whether you appear enthusiastic and positive.

Warm up your voice if you have a tendency to get nervous before interviews. Simply hum a favourite tune for a few minutes on the way to an interview to get your vocal chords working.

To ensure you speak clearly and confidently during an interview, do a further warm-up exercise by repeating a favourite phrase out loud several times. Focus on your enunciation by paying extra attention to how you use your lips and tongue to articulate every syllable. Or read a couple of paragraphs from that day's newspaper, again concentrating on using your mouth to shape the words properly.

Run mock interviews

The best way to rehearse is to ask friends or trusted acquaintances to ask you questions so you can practise responding to a real live person. Perhaps ask a friend to flick through either the index or Chapters 4 to 8 of this book to find appropriate questions to throw at you. Once you have practised the most frequently-asked interview questions, you could invite your friend to ask you questions that they have been asked in interviews so you can practise improvising.

Ask your friend to take some notes on your responses so you can evaluate them together. After the interview, you and your mock interviewer should go back over your answers and consider the questions that you may have struggled with. Ideally, you would also record your performance so you can hear what you actually said as well as observe your body language and tone of voice during the mock interview too.

Try to practise with different friends and acquaintances too. If you keep practising with only the one friend, you may find that you learn his or her personal interview style and become quite adept at performing in front of them. But at the end of the day, your interviewer is likely to be a complete stranger, so try to practise answering questions from as many different people as you can.

I realise that some people dislike role playing. But this really is the single best method for sharpening up your interview technique. So deal with your discomfort and ask as many people as you can to rehearse with you.

Ask your friend to be totally honest with you. Explain that you need them to be as critical as possible – tell them that you are not just looking for positive strokes!

IN SUMMARY ...

■ Identify and stamp out negative thoughts about yourself. Write them down and challenge them, then replace them with short, positive statements that you can repeat to yourself to buoy your confidence.

■ Use the diaphragmatic breathing technique to melt away tension.

■ Practise vivid mental visualisation to trick your brain into releasing hormones into your bloodstream that will enhance your mood and calm your nerves.

■ Practise, practise, practise. Rehearse on your own as well as with different friends and acquaintances. I really cannot overstate the importance of practising interview responses out loud!

Chapter 4

DEALING WITH COMMONLY-ASKED QUESTIONS

In this chapter ...

- **Understanding frequently-asked questions**
- **Explaining why you want the job**
- **Answering questions about your career and future direction**
- **Responding to questions about your commitment to the job**
- **Answering questions about a change of career**

Interviewers often recycle the same questions from interview to interview. Which is great news for you as a candidate because you can be sure that certain questions are likely to crop up again and again in interviews. Interviewers want to know about the decisions you have taken to get you where you are in your career, why you are looking for a new job, and why you believe you should work for them.

In answering these questions, be sure to provide brief examples whenever possible. Claims can sound like hot air if they are not substantiated with examples and evidence. Read through this chapter and remember to start jotting down some notes about how *you* would answer each question.

ANSWERING BASIC INTERVIEW QUESTIONS

Interviews often follow a certain path. Most interviewers will ask you some general questions about yourself and your career choices before plunging into more difficult questions.

Read through the following questions and be sure you can answer each one with a sharp, succinct answer that presents your skills and qualities to best possible effect.

'Tell me about yourself'

Many interviewers like to begin by asking this question. The open-ended nature of the question means that you could potentially answer it in any number of ways. So start by checking how much information the interviewer wants: 'Is there any part of my CV that you would like me to focus on?' The interviewer's response should hopefully direct you to the areas that he or she is most interested in.

If the interviewer does not give you any further guidance, stick to talking about your recent career. Imagine that the interviewer had actually asked you the question: 'Please talk me through your recent career and tell me two or three ways you think you meet our need for this job.'

Avoid talking about your upbringing, family, interests outside of work, or your goals in life. It's not wrong to talk about these – but an employer is unlikely to be impressed by them.

To prepare for this question, look at the job advert for this organisation. What skills and qualities does the advert talk about? If it says that they are looking for 'a head teacher with excellent planning and problem solving skills', then be prepared to talk about your planning and problem solving skills in your initial response.

Here are a couple of examples:

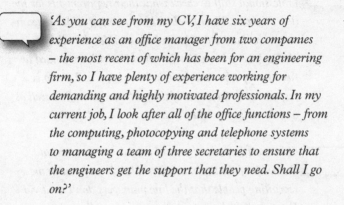

'As you can see from my CV, I have six years of experience as an office manager from two companies – the most recent of which has been for an engineering firm, so I have plenty of experience working for demanding and highly motivated professionals. In my current job, I look after all of the office functions – from the computing, photocopying and telephone systems to managing a team of three secretaries to ensure that the engineers get the support that they need. Shall I go on?'

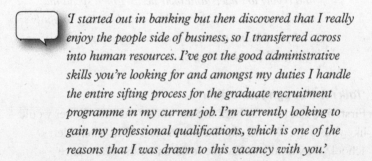

'I started out in banking but then discovered that I really enjoy the people side of business, so I transferred across into human resources. I've got the good administrative skills you're looking for and amongst my duties I handle the entire sifting process for the graduate recruitment programme in my current job. I'm currently looking to gain my professional qualifications, which is one of the reasons that I was drawn to this vacancy with you.'

'What does your day-to-day job involve?'

Rather than giving a blow-by-blow account of what you do in a typical day, you should be selective in your response. Look again at the job advert and try to figure out the key activities you will be required to do in the job and focus on those in your answer.

The two candidates from the previous question might reply by saying:

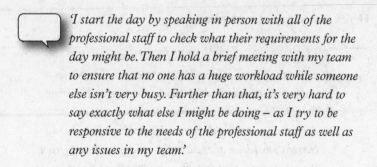

'I start the day by speaking in person with all of the professional staff to check what their requirements for the day might be. Then I hold a brief meeting with my team to ensure that no one has a huge workload while someone else isn't very busy. Further than that, it's very hard to say exactly what else I might be doing – as I try to be responsive to the needs of the professional staff as well as any issues in my team.'

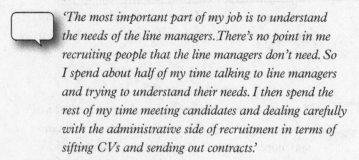

'The most important part of my job is to understand the needs of the line managers. There's no point in me recruiting people that the line managers don't need. So I spend about half of my time talking to line managers and trying to understand their needs. I then spend the rest of my time meeting candidates and dealing carefully with the administrative side of recruitment in terms of sifting CVs and sending out contracts.'

'Talk me through your career'

First, find out how far back in your career the interviewer would like you to go: 'Would you like me to start from when I left school? Or would you like me to focus on the years since I completed my degree?'

In any case, this is not an invitation to ramble at length about your career. Instead, think about how you can summarise why you left or joined each company that you have worked for. And finish off by talking about why you want to move on again.

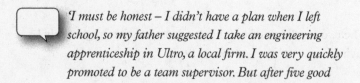

'I must be honest – I didn't have a plan when I left school, so my father suggested I take an engineering apprenticeship in Ultro, a local firm. I was very quickly promoted to be a team supervisor. But after five good

*years, I felt that I had learnt everything that I could
there, so I moved to Factory Magix, which was a much
bigger company. Now I've discovered that I really
enjoy marketing – but Factory Magix has only a small
marketing department, which brings me to this interview
with you.'*

*Practise your response to this question and time yourself.
You should avoid speaking for more than two or – at the
very most – three minutes.*

'Have you ever regretted anything about your career?'

'Regret' is a strong word – so best to avoid confessing that you
have had any serious regrets. If you must make an admission,
try to talk about a decision that happened a long time ago that
could in no way reflect badly on you in this interview.

*'I don't regret the course of my career, because I have
worked in some interesting companies and succeeded
in my chosen profession. However, I do sometimes wish
that I had taken an overseas secondment while I was
working with Medical Logistics back in the 90s when I
was young, free and single, to have had the experience of
immersing myself in another culture.'*

'What do you like/enjoy most in your job?'

Your tactic for responding to this question should be very
similar to that for dealing with the previous question about your
day-to-day job. Again, think about the main responsibilities in
the job that you are being interviewed for. Then incorporate
these into your reply.

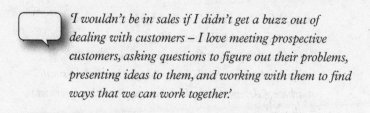

'I wouldn't be in sales if I didn't get a buzz out of dealing with customers – I love meeting prospective customers, asking questions to figure out their problems, presenting ideas to them, and working with them to find ways that we can work together.'

Ensure your body language and tone of voice convey your enthusiasm when talking about the stuff you enjoy!

'What motivates you?'

Ideally, you should be able to tell the interviewer that you are most motivated when you are helping your employer to achieve its goals. If you can, try to give a concrete example of how you succeeded in helping your employer to achieve its goals too. Consider some of these examples:

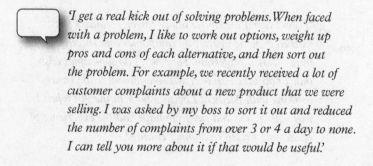

'I get a real kick out of solving problems. When faced with a problem, I like to work out options, weight up pros and cons of each alternative, and then sort out the problem. For example, we recently received a lot of customer complaints about a new product that we were selling. I was asked by my boss to sort it out and reduced the number of complaints from over 3 or 4 a day to none. I can tell you more about it if that would be useful.'

'I like to know that my work is making a difference and to be surrounded by other bright people who are also committed to the same goals. For example, in my current role, we launched a new fund-raising initiative and I got such a buzz from thinking through how we could make it happen.'

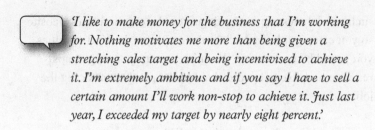

'I like to make money for the business that I'm working for. Nothing motivates me more than being given a stretching sales target and being incentivised to achieve it. I'm extremely ambitious and if you say I have to sell a certain amount I'll work non-stop to achieve it. Just last year, I exceeded my target by nearly eight percent.'

'What do you like least about your current job?'

An interviewer will not believe you if you say that you enjoy every single moment of your job. A good trick is to talk about inefficient systems, unwieldy processes or bureaucracy. However, when you do give your example, either allude to the fact that the things that frustrate you are entirely out of your control or that you have tried to improve the situation but have good reasons for not being able to change it. Even better if you can say that the situation is currently being fixed due to your efforts.

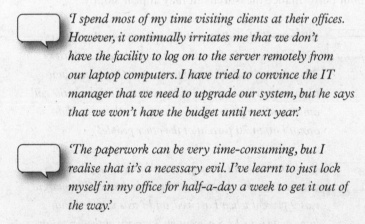

'I spend most of my time visiting clients at their offices. However, it continually irritates me that we don't have the facility to log on to the server remotely from our laptop computers. I have tried to convince the IT manager that we need to upgrade our system, but he says that we won't have the budget until next year.'

'The paperwork can be very time-consuming, but I realise that it's a necessary evil. I've learnt to just lock myself in my office for half-a-day a week to get it out of the way.'

'How do you think you'd be spending your time if we offered you the job?'

Look at the job advert as well as other sources of information such as a job description or details on the organisation's website so you can paraphrase back to the employer the kind of duties you would be performing. To finish your response, perhaps reiterate how excited you feel about the prospect of doing the job.

'My understanding is that I'd be working in shifts at the call centre and taking calls from customers and trying to answer their questions by looking up the answers on your computer system. I read on your website that on average we will have to respond to anywhere between 15 to 30 calls an hour. But as I like dealing with people and I like computers, I think it should be a great job.'

'How is your performance measured?'

Be as specific as possible in your answer. Talking about specifics makes you more believable. Candidates who are unable to talk about performance measurement may appear sloppy.

'We have daily call targets. We have to handle at least 120 inbound calls from customers and make at least 30 outbound calls to customers a day. Our individual performance is compared against that of others in the call centre and my performance is consistently better than around 60 to 70 percent of the other people.'

'I am currently measured on my ability to improve the gross margin for the products that I look after. The margin was 9 percent when I arrived, and I was targeted with improving it to 12.5 percent by January of the next year. However, I actually exceeded my target by improving the margin to 13.2 percent – which was primarily through revenue growth as opposed to cost cutting.'

In answering this question, be ready also for the likely follow-up question: 'And how are you performing against those measures?'

'How would you describe your current company?'

Some interviewers have it in their minds that a candidate that knocks a current or previous employer could be a troublemaker. It may not be fair or right – but if you want the job, you should ideally be able to give the impression that you enjoy working at your current company, but that there are just one or two aspects of your interviewer's organisation that are even more attractive.

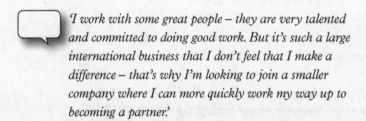 *'I work with some great people – they are very talented and committed to doing good work. But it's such a large international business that I don't feel that I make a difference – that's why I'm looking to join a smaller company where I can more quickly work my way up to becoming a partner.'*

'What have you done recently to develop yourself?'

Employers value employees who continually look to improve themselves. Ideally, try to talk about a course you are (or have) taken or a project that is expanding your skills.

'I've just started a diploma course in marketing and sales management. It will take me two years to complete, but I'm confident that it will allow me to be more effective in what I do.'

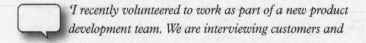 *'I recently volunteered to work as part of a new product development team. We are interviewing customers and*

*suppliers to figure out what other products we could
be manufacturing, so I am getting a lot of exposure to
customers that I wouldn't normally meet in my day-to-
day role in the back office.'*

If you are struggling to talk about a course or project, you could
probably mention a book that you are reading to improve your
skills at work. Or perhaps talk about some endeavour you are
pursuing outside of work that will develop some transferable
skill that will benefit you in your work:

*'I've just started reading a book on Total Quality
Management, which I hope will help me to boost
productivity in the team.'*

*'I'm currently spending one Saturday a month working
with a support group for the long-term unemployed.
It is giving me a great deal of exposure to people with
different backgrounds, which I hope will help me to
understand and manage my team more effectively
too.'*

'What kind of salary are you after?'

Avoid talking about this in a first interview, as you don't want to
price yourself out of the market. Nor do you want to mention a
salary that is far lower than what they might be willing to pay as
that could compromise your ability to ask for more later on.

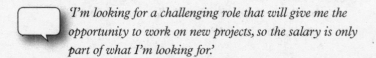

*'I'm looking for a challenging role that will give me the
opportunity to work on new projects, so the salary is only
part of what I'm looking for.'*

However, if the interviewer persists and asks you a second time, you may need to give them a rough idea – but again, without pricing yourself out of the market. Try something along the lines of:

'I'd be looking for in the region of £24,000 to £28,000 but as I said, the exact package is less important to me than finding a challenging job role. So I'd rather hold off on giving you an exact figure until I find out more about the role.'

There is more advice on how to negotiate salary in Chapter 12.

Avoid at all costs mentioning too high a salary. To get the job, you must convince the employer that you are interested in the challenge rather than just a big fat pay cheque.

'How much are you earning at the moment?'

This is a more difficult question to deflect than 'What kind of salary are you after?' because the interviewer is asking you a direct question. Give your precise salary but then, if you know that your current salary is somewhat higher than what the organisation may be able to pay, reiterate that you are most interested in finding the right organisation to join rather than the same kind of pay.

'I currently earn £37,000 basic plus bonuses. However, I understand that the salary here may be initially lower – but I'm prepared to negotiate as this role would give me the opportunity to do the bits of my job that I love the most.'

'May we check your references?'

It is natural to be concerned about having your references checked if your current employer does not know that you are looking for a job.

 'I'd be happy for you to check my references eventually, but could I please ask you to hold off for the moment? My employer doesn't know that I am currently looking for a job, so I'd rather wait until I had a firm job offer on the table before alerting them.'

If you wanted to hammer home your best points, you could finish off by telling the interviewer what you think your references might say: 'However, I know that my boss would tell you that …' and so on.

 Make sure that your references will be positive. Choose them carefully and check that your referees are happy to speak in unreservedly positive terms about you (see also Chapter 11).

TALKING ABOUT WHY YOU WANT THIS JOB

Interviewers are frequently interested to hear about the decisions that you have made in your career. Why did you take a certain job? And why *didn't* you take certain jobs?

'Why are you looking for another job?'

Three of the best reasons to mention in responding to this question are to talk about wanting to seek more challenge, greater job security, or greater rewards:

 'I've had a great time with my company. But I have

ambitions and realise that I can do more. I want to feel more stretched and so this new, bigger role is exactly what I feel I need.'

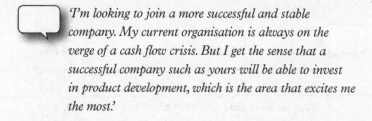

'I'm looking to join a more successful and stable company. My current organisation is always on the verge of a cash flow crisis. But I get the sense that a successful company such as yours will be able to invest in product development, which is the area that excites me the most.'

'I know that I can make a significant contribution to my employer. So rather than just earning a salary, I would like to be able to take an equity stake in a growing business.'

Try to avoid saying that you left a previous employer due to any sort of personal conflict though – for example, that you did not get on with your boss or that the company failed to give you the promotion that you wanted. Such comments could reflect badly on you – the interviewer may start to wonder whether you were in part to blame for not getting on with your boss or not being offered a promotion.

Focus on the positive reasons you want to join a new company rather than the negative reasons you want to leave another one. If you must mention negative reasons, avoid dwelling on them.

'Why do you want to leave your current employer?'

This is just a variation of the last question. Again, remember to emphasise the positive qualities of the interviewing organisation as opposed to whingeing about negative aspects of your current employment situation. For example, mentioning that your current commuting time is too long makes you sound like a moaner – so try to talk about something else.

 'I wouldn't say that I'm trying to get away at all. I enjoy the work and I have a great group of people around me. However, I've been there for nearly three years now and I feel that I've learnt most of what I'll be able to get out of that business. And when I read about this position with your company, I was excited by the prospect of working for a larger business with more scope for my personal career development.'

'Why did you leave your last employer without another job to go to?'

If you weren't made redundant from your last job, you will have to deflect the negative thrust of this question. The interviewer may be trying to get you to own up to problems that you experienced (or even caused) in your last job. Rather than take the interviewer's bait, focus your answer by talking about the positive decisions that you've had since leaving your last job.

 'We went through a restructuring and a lot changed. The direction of the overall company changed and a new manager was parachuted into our team. Also, the nature of our jobs changed, meaning that a lot of our autonomy was taken away from us. Actually two of my colleagues decided that they wanted to work elsewhere as well. I was so frustrated but also so busy that I literally did not have the time to focus on looking for a new job. Since then, however, what it has helped me to realise is the kind of environment I do want to work in. One of the main

reasons I'm so excited about the position with you is that you have chosen to focus on exactly the kind of work that was taken away from us in my old job.'

'How would you describe your ideal job?'

Don't fall into the trap of talking about what you would expect from an employer – such as the salary and benefits. Instead, talk about what you could contribute to the organisation. For instance:

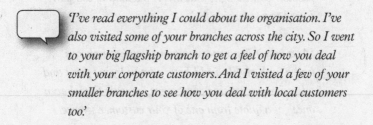

'I enjoy passing on my expertise to the people around me. I know that I can only move upwards in my career by developing the people in my team to be my successor.'

'My ideal job is one in which I have lots of autonomy in how I can meet organisational objectives. From what I've read about this job, you're looking for someone who can take on a lot of responsibility very quickly, and that sounds like a fantastic opportunity to me.'

'What do you know about our organisation?'

This question should never be a problem if you have done your research (see Chapter 1). While this may seem like a straightforward factual question, the interviewer is really looking to gauge how much research you have done on the organisation as an indicator of how seriously you want to work for them.

'I've read everything I could about the organisation. I've also visited some of your branches across the city. So I went to your big flagship branch to get a feel of how you deal with your corporate customers. And I visited a few of your smaller branches to see how you deal with local customers too.'

'My understanding from speaking to people in the industry is that your company is experiencing a squeeze on profit margins due to increased competition from aggressive American entrants into the market. However, I have experience of having grown sales and profits in my current job by over 20 percent for three years running, so I am confident that I would be able to make a contribution to the business.'

'I've had a look on your website and was most interested to read that you're launching a new model of the Z500 range next year. I also had a look at the city business library but couldn't find much written about your company, so I'd be intrigued to learn more about your growth plans and the new products you are planning for the next couple of years.'

'What do you think of our organisation?'

Your answer to this question should both demonstrate what you know about the organisation and tell the interviewer why you want to work there.

'I read on your website that you put all of your trainees on an intensive five-day training programme. I think that kind of commitment to training and development must be indicative of the importance you place in your people – so I thought that this is the kind of company I need to be working for.'

'As a major insurance company, you have always had a high profile and I have admired your print and television advertising campaigns for some time. I even once got a quote from one of your customer service

*assistants on the cost of taking out household insurance
with you and I remember thinking that the assistant was
ever so friendly and helpful. And the feeling I get is that
customer service is a very big part of what you do, which
is great as customer service is the bit of my job that I get
the most enjoyment from.'*

*'I did a six-week placement here when I was at school
so I've always been impressed by how much fun people
seemed to be having here. The people are of course
very professional but I get the feeling that the people
here would almost do the work for free. So I've always
thought that this would be a great place to work.'*

'What would you do differently if you were in charge of our organisation?'

This kind of question implies that the interviewer is looking
for an intelligent answer that shows you can make comments
that are constructively critical as opposed to simply entirely
complimentary.

*Be careful of being overly negative. To make your
criticism easier to swallow, try to offer up some positive
comments first.*

*'There's not a lot I'd do differently. The organisation has
obviously been incredibly successful over the last 20 years
since the founder started the business. I can't really say
that I'd change anything, but I have to say that I've not
noticed your organisation being mentioned in the press
as much as some of your competitors. It may be because
you've deliberately decided not to do as much publicity,*

but if I was in charge I guess that's one thing I'd want to look at.'

'What contribution could you make if we offered you a job right now?'

You're on safe ground if you repeat back the key responsibilities that were listed in the job advert for the position. Of course, the answer will differ whether you're being employed to work in the post room or as managing director of a division.

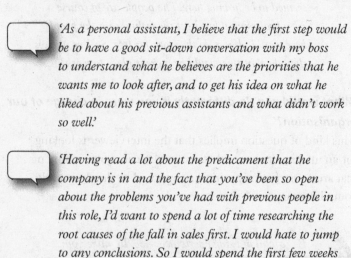

'As a personal assistant, I believe that the first step would be to have a good sit-down conversation with my boss to understand what he believes are the priorities that he wants me to look after, and to get his idea on what he liked about his previous assistants and what didn't work so well.'

'Having read a lot about the predicament that the company is in and the fact that you've been so open about the problems you've had with previous people in this role, I'd want to spend a lot of time researching the root causes of the fall in sales first. I would hate to jump to any conclusions. So I would spend the first few weeks speaking firstly with directors in the other departments and then my direct reports to get a broader picture of where they think things have gone wrong.'

'Are you familiar with our products/services/work?'

Again, good research on your part will allow you to finesse this kind of question. Remember if possible to buy or try an organisation's products or services so you can speak of them first-hand rather than purely by having read about them.

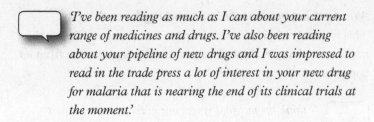

'I've been reading as much as I can about your current range of medicines and drugs. I've also been reading about your pipeline of new drugs and I was impressed to read in the trade press a lot of interest in your new drug for malaria that is nearing the end of its clinical trials at the moment.'

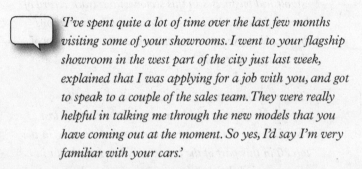

'I've spent quite a lot of time over the last few months visiting some of your showrooms. I went to your flagship showroom in the west part of the city just last week, explained that I was applying for a job with you, and got to speak to a couple of the sales team. They were really helpful in talking me through the new models that you have coming out at the moment. So yes, I'd say I'm very familiar with your cars.'

'Why do you want to work for us?'

Think about how the organisation likes to present itself to the outside world. How does this one company believe it stands out? Select a few of these unique characteristics about the organisation and incorporate them into your reply.

Many companies, for instance, believe themselves to have a good reputation or to be leaders in their field. Or the organisation may think that its employees are a breed apart from the rest.

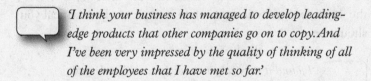

'I think your business has managed to develop leading-edge products that other companies go on to copy. And I've been very impressed by the quality of thinking of all of the employees that I have met so far.'

'What attracts you most about working for us?'

This is merely a variation on the previous question. Choose the key feature that you think differentiates the organisation from its competitors.

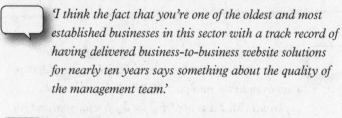

'I think the fact that you're one of the oldest and most established businesses in this sector with a track record of having delivered business-to-business website solutions for nearly ten years says something about the quality of the management team.'

'There was a survey of the most environmentally responsible construction businesses in the country last year and you were the only construction firm to be in the top 20 in this part of the country. When I read that in my research, I decided that yours is the firm I most want to work for.'

'What do you think of our website?'

This question requires a bit of a judgement call on your part. Some interviewers may simply be looking for a bit of flattery – I've known interviewers who were very proud of their websites who wanted only to hear positive comments. On the other hand, other interviewers may want to ascertain whether you can offer up constructive criticism. The best way to prepare for this question is to prepare both some positive comments and a constructively critical comment – but then to judge on the day when you're in front of an interviewer how critical you should be.

'I found it very easy to navigate and it only took me several clicks to find my way to the section on recruiting administrative staff. I also noticed that the *web designers had made the colours very striking so that older customers or people with poorer eyesight can still read it clearly. However, I don't know if it's because my computer is a bit older or not, but I did find that some of the graphics took quite a few seconds longer to download than some of your competitors. But that's a very minor criticism compared to the usefulness and accessibility of the information on there.'*

'What do you think of our app?'

Nowadays, many larger organisations have smartphone apps so it would be wise to have a view on the app created by a potential employer.

If you respond by saying something such as, 'I don't really use apps on my phone', that sends out a message that you're a bit of a dinosaur in terms of technology. Is that really the impression you want the interviewers to have of you? Even if you don't have a smartphone, at least ask a friend or member of your family to install the organisation's app so that you can see how to use it.

'What do you think of our recruitment brochure?'

As with the previous question, try to be positive about their recruitment documents and be as constructive with your criticism as possible.

'A lot of thought had obviously gone into the brochure. What I found most useful was the profiles of different people who have joined the organisation – it was useful to see that joining one particular department doesn't mean that I'll be working there forever. I also thought that it really showed off the socially responsible side of

*your organisation too, which just makes me want to work
for you even more.'*

'What worries or concerns do you have about this job?'

The best tactic for dealing with this question is to deflect the
question – certainly until after you have been made a firm offer.
Once you have been offered the job, you could always go back
to the employer to find out more about the job (see also Chapter
12 on understanding the culture of the organisation and the
nature of the work).

*'I don't have any concerns or worries about the job. But
I would like to understand more about the monthly
targets you would like me to achieve in the role and what
support you'd be able to offer to support me in achieving
them.'*

'What other jobs are you applying for?'

Interviewers most like to hear that candidates are motivated
to work in a particular field or to work in a particular role.
They worry that candidates who are applying for too wide a
range of unrelated jobs – such as a sales representative for a
pharmaceuticals firm as well as a creative job for an advertising
agency – don't know what they want to do and therefore might
not stick at the job.

*'I've applied for several other jobs but these are all in hi-
tech businesses. Technology is my big passion and that's
where I'm determined to work.'*

'How many other jobs are you applying for?'

As with the previous question, be careful about announcing too
large a number. An employer ideally wants to hear that you are

focused on a particular role or type of organisation rather than that you are applying for every job in existence.

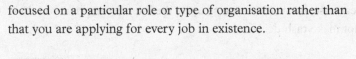 *'I've applied for jobs with the top 50 accountancy firms because I'm determined to get my business grounding through an accountancy firm.'*

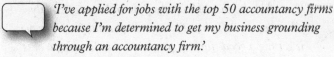 *'As I've decided that I only want to work for a top-flight graduate trainee programme, I'm applying to about a dozen companies – mostly in fast-moving consumer goods and retail. What all of these companies have in common is that they are all leaders in their fields with good brands and reputations for developing good managers.'*

'How does this job compare to other jobs you are applying for?'

In the past, interviewers could get a bit uppity when candidates admitted to having applied to more than just their company. However, in today's more mobile economy, most employers recognise that good candidates do shop around.

But a bit of a compliment about the company that is interviewing you would not go amiss – just don't overdo it.

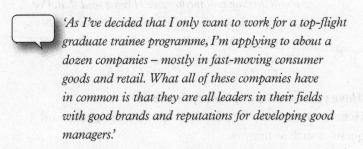 *'I have to say that the people at the other firms were also very bright. But even though this is obviously only my second interview with you, I prefer what I have heard so far about your incentive scheme.'*

'If a competitor offered you a job right now, would you accept?'

Asking this question allows interviewers to understand a little bit more about your planning and decision making skills. In your response, be sure to impress upon the interviewers that you do not make rash decisions.

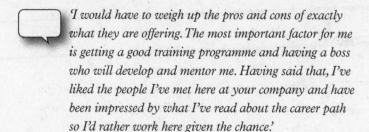

'I would have to weigh up the pros and cons of exactly what they are offering. The most important factor for me is getting a good training programme and having a boss who will develop and mentor me. Having said that, I've liked the people I've met here at your company and have been impressed by what I've read about the career path so I'd rather work here given the chance.'

'Have you received any other job offers?'

Honesty is the best policy for dealing with a straightforward question such as this.

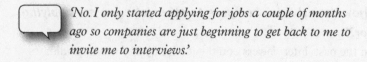

'No. I only started applying for jobs a couple of months ago so companies are just beginning to get back to me to invite me to interviews.'

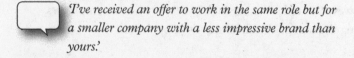

'I've received an offer to work in the same role but for a smaller company with a less impressive brand than yours.'

Avoid the temptation of lying to make yourself look like you are in demand. Your tactic could backfire as an interviewer may feel less guilty about rejecting you – thinking you have other offers to fall back on.

'How would you rate us against our competitors?'

Your research will highlight key differences between this organisation and its competitors. However, don't expect the differences to be written down anywhere for you to be able to learn and paraphrase. You may need to do quite a lot of reading and come to your own opinions as to how this organisation is different from its competitors.

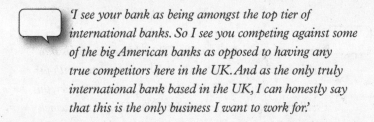

'I see your bank as being amongst the top tier of international banks. So I see you competing against some of the big American banks as opposed to having any true competitors here in the UK. And as the only truly international bank based in the UK, I can honestly say that this is the only business I want to work for.'

'You have an excellent reputation in the marketplace. Even compared with other firms such as Young Samson & Chalmers, I think that you are recognised by your clients as being truly leading edge.'

Avoid at all costs telling the interviewer how much better one of their competitors is – that may prompt the response: 'So why not go work for them then?'

'What do you know about our industry/sector?'

This question tries to ascertain how much reading and research you have done. While most candidates will have done some basic reading about the organisation, only the more exceptional candidates will tend to have read about the organisation's broader industry and sector to understand market trends.

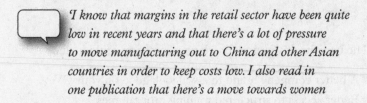

'I know that margins in the retail sector have been quite low in recent years and that there's a lot of pressure to move manufacturing out to China and other Asian countries in order to keep costs low. I also read in one publication that there's a move towards women *consumers spending less money, but on more clothing items every year, which means that they are looking for greater value rather than to trade up to more expensive clothing lines.'*

'My understanding is that moves to create an open skies agreement between the US and Europe means that airlines will now be allowed to fly between cities with far fewer constraints. While this is good for the customer, this will probably mean consolidation in the industry, which should be good news for a large airline such as yourselves with the financial firepower to buy up other smaller ones.'

'Would you rather be a big fish in a small pond or a small fish in a big pond?'

The employer wants to know whether you would rather work for a small company or a large employer. Think about what might be relevant to this particular employer.

The benefits of working in a smaller company might include:

- A greater sense of ownership in your work.
- Being able to see that you are making a visible contribution to the bottom line.
- Greater exposure to – and therefore opportunities to learn from – senior management.
- A chance to take an equity stake at an earlier stage in your career.

The benefits of working for a larger company could include:

- A better company brand that will look good on your CV.
- Better access to structured training programmes.

- Opportunities to work in offices elsewhere – perhaps even internationally.
- More financial stability and security.

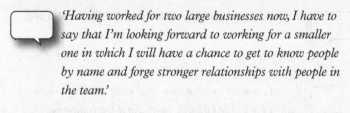

'Having worked for two large businesses now, I have to say that I'm looking forward to working for a smaller one in which I will have a chance to get to know people by name and forge stronger relationships with people in the team.'

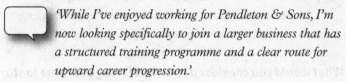

'While I've enjoyed working for Pendleton & Sons, I'm now looking specifically to join a larger business that has a structured training programme and a clear route for upward career progression.'

TALKING ABOUT YOUR FUTURE CAREER DIRECTION AND COMMITMENT

Employee turnover costs organisations money. If they decide to offer you the job, they would like to know that their investment in training you and getting you up to speed would be repaid by a good stint working for them.

'Where do you see yourself in five years' time?'

Ah, that old chestnut. If most candidates were honest, they would be forced to admit that they actually have no career plan. Unfortunately, interviewers like to hear that you have thought about the future. In your research on the organisation, try to find out what opportunities there might be for you to learn and grow or seek other opportunities within the organisation.

If the interviewer could be your future boss, it might be dangerous to say that you would like their job. However, it is increasingly acceptable for you to say that you might be ready for the next step in your career. Most employers would feel that they had got a return on their investment if you stayed for five years.

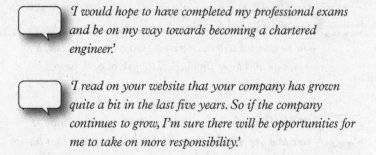

'I would hope to have completed my professional exams and be on my way towards becoming a chartered engineer.'

'I read on your website that your company has grown quite a bit in the last five years. So if the company continues to grow, I'm sure there will be opportunities for me to take on more responsibility.'

'What would you consider a reasonable length of time to stay in a job?'

A good response might be to separate out the length of time you would stay in a *job* as opposed to the time you would stay with the *organisation*.

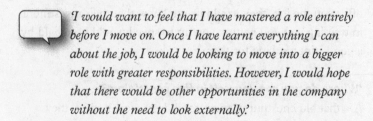

'I would want to feel that I have mastered a role entirely before I move on. Once I have learnt everything I can about the job, I would be looking to move into a bigger role with greater responsibilities. However, I would hope that there would be other opportunities in the company without the need to look externally.'

'What do you think you should be earning in three years' time?'

You need to be careful that your ambitions match the ability of the company to provide you with raises in your salary. Just as an example, a librarian in a public sector organisation is less likely to be able to double their salary than a barrister in the same period.

Make sure that your response takes into account what you understand the market would pay for someone with three more years of experience than yourself:

'My understanding is that the next level up from this role is the supervisor level. Reading on your website, I saw that the salary is around £6,000 more a year than for the role I'm applying for. As I hope to be a supervisor with you by then, that's the range I'd be aiming for.'

But perhaps the best response is to try to deflect the question and move on to another topic:

'I hope that my pay will reflect my contribution to the organisation, but the most important thing for me is having a variety of different projects to work on that will keep me employable.'

'Do you have any personal goals that you have yet to achieve?'

Even though the question asks you about personal goals, avoid talking about goals outside of your work such as wanting to get married, have children, get fit, and so on, as those could make you appear less than fully committed to your work. It is always safer to talk about a goal that would make you more valuable to your employer.

'I'm always looking to develop myself and move out of my comfort zone. As I didn't go to university, I think it would be a good idea to get a professional qualification, so that would be my next step. Hopefully, if I were to work for you, this organisation might sponsor me or at least support me in some way.'

'I would like to move into general management. I've had a lot of experience of working behind the bar and waiting on tables. But I've only had limited experience of working as a shift manager. So I see the next few years as gaining enough experience of working as a shift manager and also doing some of the behind-the-scenes administration to allow me to become a general manager.'

'What are your development objectives for the coming year?'

Be careful not to talk about having too many development objectives. 'Development objectives' could easily be taken as meaning 'development needs', i.e. weaknesses. Instead, parry this question by talking about how this job will stretch you and help you to meet your development objectives for the coming year.

 'One of my objectives has always been to move into a creative industry. While I've enjoyed my time working in the automotive industry, I think that there's more room for me to grow and develop my skills within the creative industry. So hopefully spending time in this role and getting to grips with the different challenges within your industry will stretch me enough for this year.'

'You seem to have changed jobs very frequently – why is that?'

Employers can worry that you will join and get trained up, only to move on again. So you must be ready to give a good reason for each and every one of your job moves. For example, you may have genuinely completed what you set out to do in that company – such as learning a particular skill or turning around a team before moving on to a new challenge. Or there may have been a common reason for having changed jobs several times.

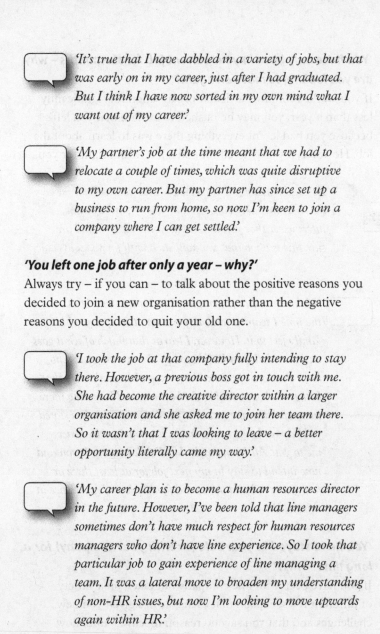

'It's true that I have dabbled in a variety of jobs, but that was early on in my career, just after I had graduated. But I think I have now sorted in my own mind what I want out of my career.'

'My partner's job at the time meant that we had to relocate a couple of times, which was quite disruptive to my own career. But my partner has since set up a business to run from home, so now I'm keen to join a company where I can get settled.'

'You left one job after only a year – why?'

Always try – if you can – to talk about the positive reasons you decided to join a new organisation rather than the negative reasons you decided to quit your old one.

'I took the job at that company fully intending to stay there. However, a previous boss got in touch with me. She had become the creative director within a larger organisation and she asked me to join her team there. So it wasn't that I was looking to leave – a better opportunity literally came my way.'

'My career plan is to become a human resources director in the future. However, I've been told that line managers sometimes don't have much respect for human resources managers who don't have line experience. So I took that particular job to gain experience of line managing a team. It was a lateral move to broaden my understanding of non-HR issues, but now I'm looking to move upwards again within HR.'

'You have only been in your current job for six months – why are you looking to move on again?'

If you worked for any particular organisation for significantly less than a year, you may be pushed to explain that you left because you had learnt everything there was to learn about the job. However, it's okay to admit that a job wasn't right for you.

Be sure to assure the interviewer that you will not make the same mistake with this job – demonstrate to this interviewer that you have done your research and are sure this is a job that you will stick with for years to come.

'I joined my current employer because I thought at the time I wanted to work for a small company with a family feel to it. However, I learnt that much of what goes on in a small firm is dictated by the two partners who have their own personal interests – they don't seem that bothered about growing the business and becoming more successful. But the fact that your organisation has stated publicly and repeatedly that it wants to grow attracts me to you. All I can say is that I've learnt my lesson and now intend to stay in my next job for at least three or four years to build up a solid foundation of experience in this field.'

'You have stayed in your role (or with your company) for a long time – why?'

If you have been with one company but taken on a variety of different roles, explain that each role has given you new challenges and that you saw no reason to leave – until now. Effectively, you should be able to argue that you genuinely had, for example, ten years of experience as opposed to one year of experience repeated ten times. Then continue with your reasons for wanting to work with this new employer:

 'Yes, I've been with this company for 15 years, but I've had a hand in an extraordinary amount of change in that time. Our client base has grown from mainly regional customers to national and even international customers now so my responsibilities have grown correspondingly. And we have gone through many technological changes that I've had to manage – from incorporating the latest design software into the business to handling the integration of the several businesses that my organisation has acquired over the years.'

It is trickier if you have been in just the one job for a long time without having been promoted. Perhaps your reasons are to do with your family:

 'I didn't want to take on a managerial role because I wanted to have an active role in bringing up our two young children. But now that they are at secondary school, I'm ready to get my career back on track by taking on new responsibilities.'

'Given you have stayed in your company for a long time, how will you cope with a new job?'

The interviewer is expressing a concern that you may struggle to make the transition to a new environment with fresh faces and different ways of working. Put the interviewer's fears to rest by providing an example of how you have made some sort of successful transition at work.

 'I've had to deal with a lot of change in my time at this

*company. Only six months ago, my company made 20
percent of our team redundant to reduce costs. However,
I was chosen to work with HR to restructure the team.
Even though it was an uncomfortable situation for a
while, I not only adapted to it, but also helped others to
adjust to it too.'*

HANDLING QUESTIONS ABOUT CHANGES IN YOUR CAREER DIRECTION

Most interviewers are more used to dealing with fresh young
school leavers or graduates than people who have decided to
change career later on in life. Such interviewers may simply
have less experience of dealing with more mature candidates –
so be ready to answer questions as to why you are considering a
departure from your current career into a new one.

'Why do you want to work in this field?'

A good response to this question should demonstrate to the
interviewers that you have thought out the pros and cons of this
career path rather than that you have stumbled into it without
thinking it through.

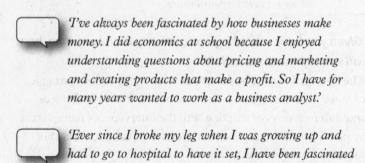

*I've always been fascinated by how businesses make
money. I did economics at school because I enjoyed
understanding questions about pricing and marketing
and creating products that make a profit. So I have for
many years wanted to work as a business analyst.'*

*'Ever since I broke my leg when I was growing up and
had to go to hospital to have it set, I have been fascinated
by hospital environments. I remember how kind and
helpful the nurses were and since then I've always*

wanted to work in nursing. The more I've read about it and talked to nurses about the ins and outs of the job, the more determined I've been to pursue this path.'

'Why do you want to change career?'

The fact that you have been invited to interview means that you may have the skills necessary to do the job. The interviewer who asks this question is probably more interested to find out your motivations and to check that you know what you are getting yourself into.

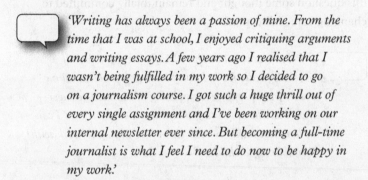

'Writing has always been a passion of mine. From the time that I was at school, I enjoyed critiquing arguments and writing essays. A few years ago I realised that I wasn't being fulfilled in my work so I decided to go on a journalism course. I got such a huge thrill out of every single assignment and I've been working on our internal newsletter ever since. But becoming a full-time journalist is what I feel I need to do now to be happy in my work.'

'It was by chance a few years ago that my boss asked me to put together the website for our company. So I had to learn to use web design packages and the programming language. And building our website was the most fun I've had in work for years. Since then, I have been helping friends to build websites to display their wedding and holiday photos – I find that the time goes by very quickly when I'm working on web design projects. And even though applying for this job with you would mean a bit of a pay cut, I know that it's what I want to do.'

When talking about your passion and determination to enter into this new profession, make sure you use your body language and tone of voice to corroborate your spoken message too.

'How do you feel about starting at the bottom of the career ladder again?'

Demonstrate in your response that you have already given this question some thought and remain totally committed to changing career direction.

'I feel fine about it as I've already prepared myself psychologically for it. I don't have any problem taking orders from people who are going to be much younger than me. The only thing that matters to me is that I can at long last fulfil my ambition of retraining to work with disadvantaged children.'

'How are you going to cope with the drop in salary?'

Again, use your answer to show the interviewers that you have already thought through the financial implications of doing something new.

'I've already read in your recruitment literature about the salary that is on offer and it's a sum that I can put up with for the moment. Eventually I hope that my added experience will allow me to make a larger contribution to the organisation and therefore help me to progress quite quickly up the ranks.'

Make sure you really can survive and support yourself and/or your family on your new salary. Have you calculated the impact on your finances of taking home less money?

'How do we know this change of career won't just be a passing phase?'

Try to construct an answer that shows the time and effort you have already invested in researching your new career choice.

'I hope that what I've already done in the last year should demonstrate how committed I am to becoming a veterinary nurse. Studying for and passing my Level 2 Certificate for Animal Nursing Assistants while carrying on with my full-time job has obviously been challenging. Plus I took it upon myself to find two work placements so that I could get some practical experience of working alongside veterinary staff so I am confident that I have a solid appreciation of the demands of the job now.'

'How would you feel if you couldn't work in this field?'

Be positive and demonstrate to the employers that you aren't willing to give up your goal of working in this new field or profession.

'It's not something I'm willing to consider. I've already demonstrated my commitment by taking some of the required courses through home study and I'm going to be ready to take my first exam next month. If I get rejected this time round, I shall have to wait until applications open again next year to try again. But by then I will

*have gained further exam qualifications and I will also
continue to pursue opportunities to do voluntary work in
this area so that I can strengthen my CV.'*

IN SUMMARY...

■ Read through the questions in this chapter and think about
how you would respond to each of them.

■ Tailor your answers so that what you say ties in exactly with
the skills that each employer is looking for. The answer you
give one organisation may necessarily have to be different
from the answer you give another organisation.

■ Be ready to talk about the reasons behind each of the career
decisions that you have ever made. And be prepared to talk
about your career future, remembering that you should try to
impress upon the interviewers your willingness to commit for
some number of years, too.

■ If you're changing careers entirely, be sure you can assure
the interviewer that you have given the matter a lot of
consideration and are ready for all of the psychological,
practical, and financial aspects of doing so.

Chapter 5

TALKING ABOUT YOUR PERSONAL QUALITIES

In this chapter …
- **Talking in general terms about yourself**
- **Demonstrating your ability to get work done**
- **Dealing with hypothetical questions**

You can't blame interviewers for asking lots of questions.
There's a lot at stake for them. They want to make sure they can
hire someone who is right for the job, who will be able to do the
job well and help the team and broader organisation to succeed.
They don't want to end up hiring someone who will turn out
to be a slacker, bungling idiot, or clever rocket scientist with no
people skills.

This chapter deals with the many questions that interviewers
may ask you about your skills, your personality, and your
motivations. As you read this chapter, remember to keep making
notes as to how *you* would answer each question though.

DESCRIBING YOURSELF IN POSITIVE TERMS

Responding to questions that ask you to rate yourself or to
evaluate yourself as others see you need to be handled with
some subtlety. When talking about what you bring to an
employer, there is a fine line between confidence and arrogance,
so tread carefully. Similarly, when talking about your negative
points and weaknesses, very little separates being sufficiently
honest with being foolishly candid.

'What is your greatest strength?'

From your analysis of the job advert, you should by now have figured out the key skills that are required for this particular role. So answering the question should be a breeze. If you can, talk about how one of your strengths is one of the key skills they are looking for.

 Remember to offer a brief example of how you have used your strength at work in order to hammer your point home.

 'I'm good at keeping calm when others are getting stressed. For example, a customer rang our team saying that an order had got lost along the way. Some of my colleagues were getting panicky about what to do so I called a meeting and we brainstormed ideas and decided to hire a pick-up van that afternoon to drive a replacement batch of our product to the customers ourselves.'

 'I think that my greatest strength is my ability to take in complex company financial information, build a spreadsheet to analyse its profitability, and make a decision very quickly as to whether the company would be a good venture or not. Recently I did that for an Eastern European business that my boss was thinking about buying and I completed the financial valuation of it in a single weekend.'

'What is your greatest weakness?'

If you get asked about your strengths, you *will* get asked about your weaknesses or development needs. However, candidates who are unable to come up with any weaknesses at all are often viewed with suspicion – are you claiming to be superhumanly perfect? Rather than say you have no weaknesses (which interviewers are more likely to interpret as arrogance on your part), choose a couple of minor weaknesses that are unrelated to your ability to do the job. For example, if your job is only to implement other people's ideas, you could say that you aren't very good at coming up with your own ideas.

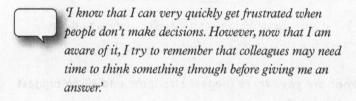

'I know that I can very quickly get frustrated when people don't make decisions. However, now that I am aware of it, I try to remember that colleagues may need time to think something through before giving me an answer.'

'I like to be quite autonomous in my work. Years ago, I had a very controlling boss who wanted to sit down with me and tell me exactly how to do every little task. But that's not happened in my last few jobs and from what I understand of this role, I'm going to be working quite independently so I know it's not going to be a problem here either.'

But don't try to turn your weaknesses into strengths. Two examples that seem to come up are: 'One of my weaknesses is that I'm a bit of a perfectionist – I tend to spend longer than necessary making sure that things are perfect.' When I hear a candidate mention that, I just think that they've read it from a book. Another poor example of a weakness to cite is: 'You might say I don't suffer fools gladly – I can't tolerate poor quality or lack of effort from other people'. Again, it sounds too rehearsed and implies that the candidate lacks any self-awareness about themselves.

> *If you mention any weaknesses that could affect your ability to do the job, be ready to describe what actions you are taking to improve or develop yourself.*

'What is your greatest area for development?'

There are many euphemisms for weaknesses. So be ready to answer the same question under different guises such as:

- 'What are your development needs with respect to this role?'
- 'What is your greatest area of under-strength?'

'What are your three biggest strengths and three biggest weaknesses?'

Just a variation on the basic strengths and weaknesses questions. It pays to plan ahead to have at least three or four strengths up your sleeve and a similar number of weaknesses in case the interviewer insists on a certain number.

'How would your colleagues/team/boss describe you?'

Although you may be tempted to present a rounded picture of how your colleagues see you – you should try to get away with treating this question as if you had been asked, 'What would your colleagues say are your strengths?' There is no benefit in mentioning weaknesses unless the interviewer specifically asks for them.

Simply talk about two or three of the key skills that are required of the job. For example, a gym instructor being interviewed for a job at a health club might say:

> *'I think that my colleagues would say that I am very client-focused. I don't just stand around, waiting for*

members of the gym to come and ask me questions.
I wander around the gym, observing how they are
getting on, chatting and offering advice. In fact, when
the members of the gym were asked to rate the five
instructors in the gym, I got a 4.5 rating out of 5.'

If you can though, try to back up your claims with any
objective evidence that you may have on how colleagues
have described you – such as from an appraisal or from a
360-degree feedback report.

'Of course we all focus on the positives, but if I asked your colleagues/team/boss to be picky, what would they say your faults are?'

This may be a follow-on question from a tricky interviewer.
Treat this question as if the interviewer had asked you to talk
about your weaknesses (see earlier on in this chapter).

'What would your friends say your biggest fault is?'

The trick here is to pick a weakness that applies only to your
personal life and could never interfere with your work life.

'I suppose they might say that I'm a bit of an impulse
shopper. I really like technology and gadgets. I like to
understand how they work so I end up buying toys for
myself that I don't really need.'

'How would your rate yourself as…?'

You could be asked to rate yourself as a team player, a
researcher, a leader, or just about anything else. Obviously you
need to start by saying that you are a very good team player,
researcher, leader, etc. – don't let modesty get in the way of

making a good impression on the interviewer. But the secret then is to back up your assertion with a short example that demonstrates that you are as good as you say.

Be careful not to make overly extravagant claims about yourself unless you have evidence to support it – such as having won an award, being specifically praised by a colleague, or having received the biggest bonus amongst your peer group.

'I'd say that I was one of the best technicians in our company. For example, we get a set of ratings in our annual appraisal. I was the only technician to get awarded the top ranking in four out of the six skill categories and the second best ranking in the remaining two.'

'I'd rate myself as a good leader because I work hard at developing the capability of the people who work for me. Just a few months ago, one of my team was promoted. She used to be very shy but I spent a lot of time coaching her and building her confidence in meetings – and now she's going to work in our New York office.'

'What unique skills would you bring to our company?'

A tricky question, as the interviewer is effectively asking you what you have that the other candidates do not have. If you know that you have some technical skills that very few candidates have, this is your opportunity to talk about them. However, if you are not sure that you have any skills that are unique to you and no one else, you could try a different approach – talk about the fact that you possess a combination of skills and determination that, taken together, are unique.

'I'm good with technology, but I think what makes me different is that I'm also a people person. I'm not the kind of guy who likes to sit in a room and just work on technical problems all day – I like to get out in front of customers and understand their problems and see how I can fix them.'

TALKING ABOUT YOUR ABILITY TO GET WORK DONE

At the end of the day, an interviewer is most interested in whether you can deliver results. Can you complete projects, deal with daily tasks, work with other people and on your own?

For example, teams are supposed to create something that is greater than the sum of their parts. But can you show the interviewer that you can navigate the minefield of disagreements, politicking and outright arguments that happen in most teams? On the other hand, although employers appreciate the ability to work with other people, it goes without saying that you need to demonstrate that you are able to work on your own without continual guidance and reassurance too.

'Would you say that you have good influencing skills?'

Of course say: 'Yes.' However, it is very difficult to convince an interviewer of your influencing skills if you speak about them only in abstract terms. So continue by providing an example of how you influenced someone as proof of your skill.

'Yes. For example, there was a situation a few months ago when the head of my department said that we didn't have enough money to upgrade our systems. So I took it upon myself to write a business case about the

benefits of the upgrade and I set up a meeting with the department head. He was initially quite sceptical, but when I explained it to him he understood that the new system was actually going to save us quite a lot of time and make us money in a period of only 18 months.'

'Are you a good team player?'

Of course you're a great team player. But give an example to demonstrate how you helped the team to achieve its goals.

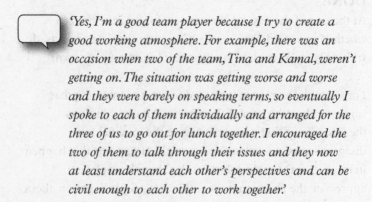

'Yes, I'm a good team player because I try to create a good working atmosphere. For example, there was an occasion when two of the team, Tina and Kamal, weren't getting on. The situation was getting worse and worse and they were barely on speaking terms, so eventually I spoke to each of them individually and arranged for the three of us to go out for lunch together. I encouraged the two of them to talk through their issues and they now at least understand each other's perspectives and can be civil enough to each other to work together.'

'I try to be a good team player by checking on the workloads of other people and ensuring that everyone's happy. Recently I noticed that one of my colleagues, Ruth, was being a lot quieter than usual. I took her aside and found out that her uncle had just died – she had just found out on the telephone and she was really shaken up. So I suggested that she ask our boss for the rest of the day off and I offered to finish off the few phone calls that she was supposed to be handling for the rest of the day.'

'What role do you tend to play within a team?'

Before you answer this question, try to think about the kind of role that you might need to assume if you were to be taken on by the employer. Don't try to tell every employer that you tend to be the leader if they are looking only for followers.

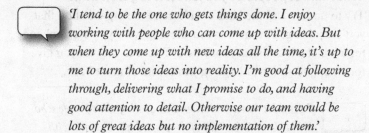

'I tend to be the one who gets things done. I enjoy working with people who can come up with ideas. But when they come up with new ideas all the time, it's up to me to turn those ideas into reality. I'm good at following through, delivering what I promise to do, and having good attention to detail. Otherwise our team would be lots of great ideas but no implementation of them.'

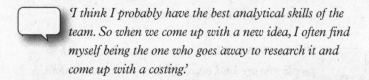

'I think I probably have the best analytical skills of the team. So when we come up with a new idea, I often find myself being the one who goes away to research it and come up with a costing.'

Try to relate the role you tend to play within a team to the role that you think the employer may need you to play within their team.

'What kind of people do you get on best with?'

The interviewer may be trying to figure out whether you will fit in with the existing team. Avoid ruling yourself out of the running by being too specific about the kinds of people you get on with.

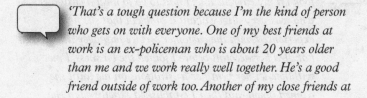

'That's a tough question because I'm the kind of person who gets on with everyone. One of my best friends at work is an ex-policeman who is about 20 years older than me and we work really well together. He's a good friend outside of work too. Another of my close friends at

work is a young single mother of two kids and we always have a laugh while we get on with our work.'

'What kind of people do you tend not to get on with?'

Try to understand the kind of culture of the organisation that you are joining. The answer you should give if you are applying for a job at a local library may be different to the one you give for an application to a large aggressive investment bank.

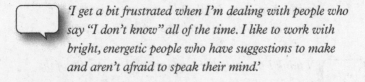

'I get a bit frustrated when I'm dealing with people who say "I don't know" all of the time. I like to work with bright, energetic people who have suggestions to make and aren't afraid to speak their mind.'

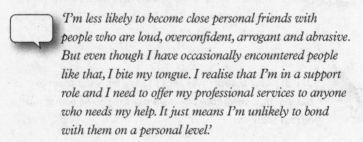

'I'm less likely to become close personal friends with people who are loud, overconfident, arrogant and abrasive. But even though I have occasionally encountered people like that, I bite my tongue. I realise that I'm in a support role and I need to offer my professional services to anyone who needs my help. It just means I'm unlikely to bond with them on a personal level.'

'How good are you at handling conflict?'

Give an example of how you have handled a tricky situation with tact and diplomacy:

'I'm good at defusing conflict. For instance, when I took on my current role, I had to go to meet a customer who was very angry about a problem that she had experienced with the customer service manager who had handled her account before I joined the business. I met with her, let her vent her frustrations on me until she calmed down and then I established exactly what she

wanted to do about the situation. That was six months ago and now she's incredibly happy with the service we provide and has increased the size of her orders by nearly 50 percent.'

'I try to avoid conflict if I can. But a couple of months ago, one of my colleagues, John, thought I was ignoring him because I was simply too busy to return his phone calls. Another colleague told me about the problem so I took John out for a coffee and we talked it through. I apologised for not appearing to want to help with the report that he wanted me to do for him and explained that I'd been spending a lot of time at our other location. It was a good conversation though and we patched things up.'

'Do you enjoy speaking in front of other people?'

The job you are applying for may not require that you stand up and give formal presentations in front of hundreds of people. But many jobs may require you to give short talks or informal updates to members of your team or department.

'Yes, I quite like speaking my mind in front of others. I got a lot of practice at college because we used to have to give ten-minute presentations to the other people in our class on our thoughts on the essay topic of the week.'

'How do you respond to personal criticism?'

You need to show the interviewer that you can take constructive criticism without taking offence or reacting defensively to it.

'As long as the criticism is fair and constructive, I try to listen to it, thank them for their candid feedback, and modify my future behaviour accordingly.'

'Can you describe a situation in which you were criticised?'

This is a natural follow-up to the previous question on how you respond to personal criticism. Avoid giving an example that involves lateness, absenteeism or aggressive behaviour – as these can signal to the interviewer that you are a troublesome employee. Better examples are to do with skills – such as presentation or computing skills – that you may have lacked at one point in your career, but which you have since worked on and had some success in improving.

'I never thought it was terribly important to understand budgets and how the business makes money. But my boss suggested that I sit down with the finance manager regularly, who was really instrumental in helping me to navigate a profit and loss account. It was hard at first but I now have a good grasp of how different costs can affect our profit margins.'

'How do you handle rejection?'

Some jobs – for example, most jobs that involve an element of selling to clients or customers – may involve more than a bit of rejection. Be sure to reassure the interviewer that you have a thick skin and don't take rejection personally.

'I never let rejection get to me. If a customer doesn't buy from me, I just pick up the phone and dial another one. I know that there are literally thousands of possible customers out there, and it's my job to talk them through the opportunities that I can offer them. The fact that I get to talk to so many varied people is one of the reasons why I enjoy selling.'

'How will you cope working with people from different backgrounds to you?'

You may have heard a lot of employers talk about the need for people to respect diversity in cultural, ethnic, gender, and other differences. So variations on this question could ask you how you work with people from 'very different educational backgrounds', 'different cultures', or 'different countries'. Whatever form the question takes, the best way to answer this is to provide an example to show that you can work with people who are very different from yourself. If you can, try also to emphasise that you not only had a good working relationship but also became good friends.

Use whatever example you have. Even if you have not worked with people from different countries or cultures, perhaps your boss was much younger than you, a colleague was a single parent with a very different view on life to you, or you worked alongside a team of scientists, actuaries, or lecturers who were all much more highly qualified than you were.

'When I transferred up to our head office, I found myself working with a lot of the sales and marketing people. I have to say that I thought they didn't really respect the people who worked in the field and didn't take my views seriously. But I worked hard to earn their respect and invested a lot of time meeting with them on a one-to-one basis. It probably took me a good six months, but now I'm pleased to say that they treat me as an equal.'

'How do you respond to authority?'

If an interviewer is asking you this question, it might be because the organisation is quite hierarchical – each employee knows their level and there might be rules on how you deal with people who are more senior than yourself.

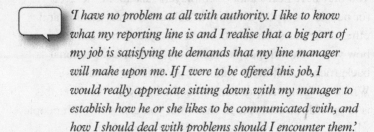

'I have no problem at all with authority. I like to know what my reporting line is and I realise that a big part of my job is satisfying the demands that my line manager will make upon me. If I were to be offered this job, I would really appreciate sitting down with my manager to establish how he or she likes to be communicated with, and how I should deal with problems should I encounter them.'

'What was the greatest failing of your boss?'

Speaking ill of your previous boss could reflect badly on you – so resist the temptation to talk at length about his or her faults. Try deflecting the question by emphasising the good qualities of your boss.

'I can't say that there is much wrong with my boss – she has a lot of experience and has coached me in many ways, especially in my ability to present confidently in front of large groups of people.'

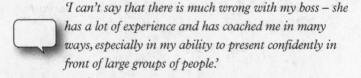

If an interviewer pursues the matter and asks for a weakness, be sure to finish off your response by talking about how you compensated for their weakness.

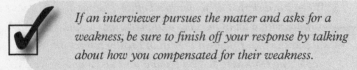

'I wouldn't say that this is a major fault – it's more of a minor quibble. My current boss can be quite forgetful. Often, you can tell him something and he can forget it even in the same day. So I have learned not to rely on him to remember times and dates of meetings. Instead, I always send him an email and send a copy to his secretary, so that she can politely manage his schedule.'

Then perhaps reinforce the fact that you had a good relationship with your boss by finishing with another positive statement – 'but this relatively minor weakness was far outweighed by the fact that she gave me a lot of responsibility' or 'but I don't want to blow this weakness out of proportion, as he also taught me a lot about project management and writing press releases.'

'Do you prefer to work on your own or with other people?'

You do not want to give the impression that you are capable of only one but not the other. However, the 'right' answer depends on the nature of the job. Before the interview, you should have figured out whether you would be spending most of your time working on your own or in a team with other people. As such, your answer should depend very much on the situation.

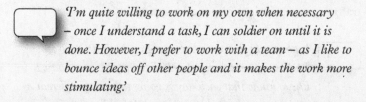

'I'm quite willing to work on my own when necessary – once I understand a task, I can soldier on until it is done. However, I prefer to work with a team – as I like to bounce ideas off other people and it makes the work more stimulating.'

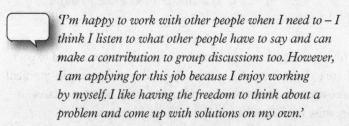

'I'm happy to work with other people when I need to – I think I listen to what other people have to say and can make a contribution to group discussions too. However, I am applying for this job because I enjoy working by myself. I like having the freedom to think about a problem and come up with solutions on my own.'

'Would you say that you are reliable?'

Of course you should say that you are reliable. However, you need to be able to give a response that makes you stand out from the other candidates. Employers worry about lateness, absenteeism from work, and forgetfulness. As a consequence, punctuality, dependability and a willingness to work overtime to meet deadlines are valued traits.

'There used to be five of us running the helpdesk. We were supposed to open at 9.00am for queries, but we also provided early cover from 7.30am. I'm proud to say that in the two-and-a-half years I worked there, I didn't miss any of my early shifts – I always either turned up or managed to swap my shift with someone else beforehand.'

'Can you work under pressure?'

Before answering this question, you need to figure out how much pressure you think the job entails. For example, a journalist for a daily newspaper, a financial trader, or an air traffic controller might respond by saying:

'I positively thrive on pressure. I couldn't do a job where I had to sit and watch the clock ticking by every day. I like to know that each day is going to be very different with its own set of decisions to make and problems to solve.'

However, if you are applying for a job where you would expect there to be more order in your day and less moment-to-moment pressure, you might want to talk a bit about how you plan and organise in order to avoid last-minute crunches:

'I sit down and look at my workload at the start of each week in order to figure out which tasks I need to do on which days. And I use a Gantt chart to keep up-to-date with projects that I am working on. However, when

things do occasionally hit the fan, I resign myself to the fact that it might be a late night in the office.'

'How do you unwind and deal with stress?'

This differs from the previous question on whether you can handle pressure, because it is asking you how you deal with the tension that can result from tight deadlines and tough days at work.

However, bear in mind that what is socially acceptable in one organisation may be deemed inappropriate by another firm – for example an aggressive sales team might snigger at candidates who profess to meditating or enjoying quiet reading. Of course such attitudes are not fair, but I'm afraid that interviewers can be prejudiced as much as anyone. So this is where your research into the culture and prevailing attitudes into the company will help you.

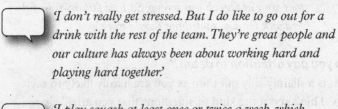

Avoid talking about the fact that you may relax by drinking alone at home – even if it's just a single glass of wine. An uptight interviewer may view this in a negative light.

'I don't really get stressed. But I do like to go out for a drink with the rest of the team. They're great people and our culture has always been about working hard and playing hard together.'

'I play squash at least once or twice a week, which really helps me to unwind and get ready for another day at work.'

'How do you cope with disappointment?'

Show that you can recover from setbacks, dust yourself off, and carry on regardless. Interviewers want to hire people who are persistent and possess tenacity and determination.

'I don't take anything personally. My view is that you have to knock on 100 doors to find the one that will open. For instance, when my boss didn't like an idea of mine that related to the way we send out invoices, I kept going back to the drawing board to refine my ideas and to ask other people across the organisation for help in tweaking them. I went back to my boss three times before she agreed to try my new invoicing method. If I get offered the job, I'm sure she'll mention what a success that was in the reference she gives me.'

'How do you deal with failure?'

Again, in answering this question, try to show that you have a positive approach to your work.

'I don't really think in terms of failure. I only think that failing to achieve something the first time around shows that your approach was wrong. So I see failure as useful feedback for how something should work.'

'Do you pay attention to detail?'

This is a slightly silly question as you are hardly likely to say, 'No.' Think about the kind of situations that you are likely to need to pay close attention to detail if you were to be offered the job. Try to construct an example of how you used your skill with detail in a similar situation in the past.

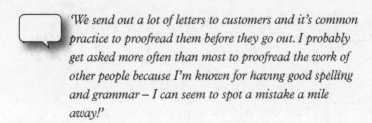

'We send out a lot of letters to customers and it's common practice to proofread them before they go out. I probably get asked more often than most to proofread the work of other people because I'm known for having good spelling and grammar – I can seem to spot a mistake a mile away!'

'How much experience do you have of managing budgets?'

Given that most organisations are looking to keep costs low, this is an opportunity for you to shine if you have had such experience. In your response, talk about the biggest budget that you have managed and be specific about how you handled it.

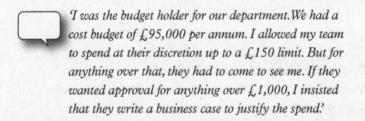

'I was the budget holder for our department. We had a cost budget of £95,000 per annum. I allowed my team to spend at their discretion up to a £150 limit. But for anything over that, they had to come to see me. If they wanted approval for anything over £1,000, I insisted that they write a business case to justify the spend.'

'How are you with new technology?'

If you are applying for a technical job, then be prepared to talk about the technical wizardry that you can extract from your systems – special functions you can use, macros that you have written, speed dials that you have devised, or shortcuts that you regularly employ.

However, most employers are more interested in basic computer literacy. In particular, employers worry that older candidates may struggle with even the basics of using a computer or other systems such as voicemail.

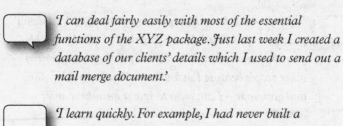

'I can deal fairly easily with most of the essential functions of the XYZ package. Just last week I created a database of our clients' details which I used to send out a mail merge document.'

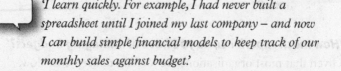

'I learn quickly. For example, I had never built a spreadsheet until I joined my last company – and now I can build simple financial models to keep track of our monthly sales against budget.'

If you have particular experience of particular software programmes that might be important in the role you're applying for, be ready to talk about the sort of tasks that you can do with them too.

'Do you use Facebook and/or Twitter?'

Privately, you may feel that you don't have the time or inclination to use social networking sites such as Facebook, Twitter or whatever else might be growing in popularity. However, be careful about revealing your preferences.

Interviewers sometimes worry that older candidates (and that could mean anyone out of their 20s!) are less flexible or perhaps less adaptable when it comes to learning about new ways of working and new technology. Saying something like, 'Oh, I can't be bothered with Facebook' could simply reinforce an interviewer's view that you might be too old and stubborn for the job.

As part of your job preparation, it might be wise to spend at least a few hours registering for the most popular social networking sites and getting to grips with them. That way, you would be able to answer at least basic questions about them in order to show that you are the kind of person who enjoys learning about new things in the world.

'How is your absenteeism / attendance record?'

You will have to be honest here, as this is something that many employers check when they ask for references. If you have had a problem, then give a good reason to explain why it occurred at the time – and why it will not happen again.

'I did have to take several months off due to a back injury I picked up while doing DIY about two years ago. But I got back to full health over a year ago and I have not had any problems since – and it's something that my references will confirm too.'

'How is your time keeping?'

No employer wants to hire someone who is going to turn up late for work and meetings all of the time.

'I'm someone who is very careful about time. I hate being late so I always find myself leaving a lot of time to get to meetings and so on. I invariably find myself arriving a lot earlier than I need to.'

'Ours is a long-hours culture – is that a problem for you?'

This may be a trick question – what they call long hours might not be what you consider to be long (or vice versa). This is the kind of trick that you should be prepared for by researching and reading up on the company. However, if you're not sure what constitutes long hours in the mind of the interviewer, ask the question: 'What exactly do you call long hours?' And then tailor your answer accordingly:

'I understand that this is a demanding job that I am applying for. But I really do thrive on the challenge of this sort of work – so I am willing to work whatever hours it takes to get the work done.'

If you have worked similarly long hours in the past, you should definitely cite this experience as well.

HANDLING HYPOTHETICAL QUESTIONS

Interviewers sometimes ask 'what if…?' and 'how would you…?' questions. Again, they are trying to see whether your approach to situations matches what they think is the right answer.

These questions can be tricky if you haven't planned a response. But just a little preparation can help you to ace them with ease.

'How would you respond to change?'

'Change management' continues to be a big buzzword at work, as organisations continually revamp how they operate in order to compete more effectively. The pace of change in the world has quickened since the start of the 21st century and only seems to be getting quicker. So employers want to hear that you are adaptable and flexible to change.

 'Some people see change as threatening. But I see change as exciting. In fact, I get bored if I'm asked to do exactly the same thing month after month. I actively enjoy pursuing new opportunities and often end up volunteering for new projects and initiatives.'

To strengthen your argument, you could go on to give an

example of how you have been involved in making change happen in the past:

> *'Last year we had a team of management consultants who helped us with a big change programme that involved restructuring the organisation and changing a lot of how we worked on a daily basis. I volunteered to join the internal consulting team to manage the relationship with the consultants and worked with them for six months.'*

'What action would you take if you disagreed with the decision of your manager?'

Saying that you would immediately speak up could mark you out as a troublemaker. So couch your response carefully.

> *'I would speak up. But there are times when tact is required – for example, if my manager were to say something in a meeting that I felt was wrong, I would wait until we had a moment alone to try to put him right. At the end of the day though, I recognise that a manager is entitled to make decisions that I may not always agree with. As long as I feel that I have been given a fair chance to air my views, I would have to go along with their decision.'*

Naturally, an interviewer may ask you for a specific example of when this might have happened too.

> *Avoid saying that you would automatically go along with your manager's wishes. You would not want the interviewer to think you would agree to do anything that breaks the rules.*

'If you spotted a colleague doing something unethical or illegal, what would you do?'

The interviewer is not asking you what you would do if your colleague were doing something that you merely disagreed with – ethics and legality are in a bigger league than mere differences of opinion. You must state that you would act immediately to put a stop to any unethical or illegal activity.

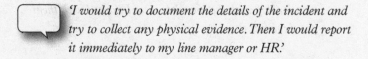

'I would try to document the details of the incident and try to collect any physical evidence. Then I would report it immediately to my line manager or HR.'

'What would you do if a colleague came to you in tears?'

Your answer should recognise that support for your colleagues can come in various forms. Listening skills and empathy are as important as being able to offer practical assistance.

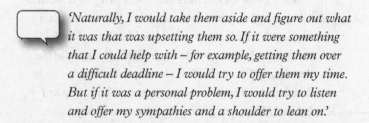

'Naturally, I would take them aside and figure out what it was that was upsetting them so. If it were something that I could help with – for example, getting them over a difficult deadline – I would try to offer them my time. But if it was a personal problem, I would try to listen and offer my sympathies and a shoulder to lean on.'

'What would you do if your partner phoned you to tell you that your son or daughter had been taken ill in the middle of the day?'

An interviewer is being a bit naughty here because recent government legislation prohibits employers from asking questions about childcare (see Chapter 7). However, many interviewers may simply not know any better about the changes in the law. So my personal approach would be to tell the interviewer what they want to hear. This is a hypothetical question, so give a hypothetical answer.

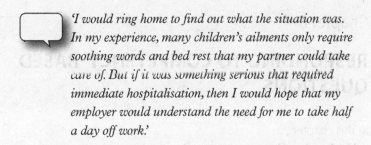

'I would ring home to find out what the situation was. In my experience, many children's ailments only require soothing words and bed rest that my partner could take care of. But if it was something serious that required immediate hospitalisation, then I would hope that my employer would understand the need for me to take half a day off work.'

'If I told you that you're not suitable for this job, what would you do?'

In reality, you may feel like throttling the interviewer with an item of his or her own clothing after all the effort you have put into preparing for the interview. However, a tactic that is more likely to get you the job may be to say:

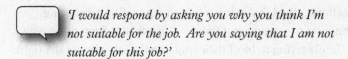

'I would respond by asking you why you think I'm not suitable for the job. Are you saying that I am not suitable for this job?'

Hopefully then, the interviewer should tell you about their concerns, allowing you to respond to each of these in turn.

IN SUMMARY...

■ Think about what the employer is looking for before you answer questions about your strengths and weaknesses.

■ Emphasise your team qualities as well as your ability to get a job done by yourself.

■ Try to answer hypothetical questions by giving a concrete example whenever possible.

Chapter 6

RESPONDING TO COMPETENCY-BASED QUESTIONS

In this chapter …
- **Understanding competencies**
- **Giving strong examples**
- **Unpeeling the layers beneath competency-based questions**
- **Using action words in your answers**
- **Answering competency-based questions with flair**

Increasingly, employers are using 'competency-based' (also sometimes called 'behavioural' or 'situational') interviewing techniques to separate out the good candidates from those who are simply trying to bluff their way into the job without the right skills or experience.

Competencies are simply an elaborate term often used by organisations to describe 'behaviours that are linked to success at work'. In other words, competencies are the key skills that the organisation is looking for in employees.

Many organisations have spent time thinking about the skills that they want all of their employees to have. Whatever the exact duties of your job, whether you are applying to be a social worker, a management consultant, an insurance clerk, or airline cabin crew – employers will almost always be looking for people who are self-motivated, can solve problems, and have good people skills.

SPOTTING COMPETENCY-BASED QUESTIONS

The theory behind competency-based interviewing is that past behaviour is the best predictor of future job performance. Putting it another way, candidates who have succeeded at certain tasks in the past will be more likely to succeed at them in the future.

As such, you can always spot competency-based interview questions because an interviewer will ask you questions about how you tackled real problems in the past. Rather than asking you about how you *generally* go about confronting issues or how you might deal with *hypothetical* scenarios, these sorts of questions ask you about *actual* situations you have faced.

Occasionally, an interviewer may actually tell you that they will be asking you competency-based questions. But in any case, competency-based questions are fairly easy to spot. They always ask about situations you experienced in the past. And they start off with phrases like:

■ 'Give me an example of…'
■ 'Can you think of an occasion when you have…?'
■ 'Tell me about a situation where you…'
■ 'Describe an instance when…'
■ 'Talk me through a time you…'

UNDERSTANDING THE KEY PRINCIPLES OF ANSWERING COMPETENCY-BASED QUESTIONS

In responding to competency-based questions, the most important principle is to: *Talk through a real example that actually happened to you.* Don't talk in broad terms about how you generally tackle those sorts of situations.

Remember, remember, remember *to talk about a* specific *example that you actually experienced!*

Once you have talked about your example, an interviewer may ask you further questions to get a deeper understanding of what you did. So, the second key principle is: *Be ready to talk about your example in a lot of detail.*

Competency-based questions help interviewers to catch out candidates who have exaggerated their skills or experience. A candidate who is trying to bluff their way into a job will be comfortable talking about their experience only at a broad level and not in any detail. So a skilled competency-based interviewer may ask for a lot of detail around each question.

Imagine for a moment the following scenario. You are a police officer and have arrested a suspect that you think burgled a house at 9.35pm on Friday 15th July. Your first question might be: 'Where were you at 9.35pm on Friday 15th July?' – to which the suspect replies that he was 'alone at home, watching television.' In order to catch him out, you might want to ask further questions such as: 'What were you watching?' Perhaps the suspect might say that he was watching his favourite soap opera. Again, to try to uncover his lying, you might ask: 'So what was happening in that particular episode?'

Now think of the interviewer as a police officer – and you, the candidate, as a suspect. The interviewer is trying to uncover whether you really used a particular skill or not. Interview candidates who are overstating their experience will not have the background information or be able to talk about their experience in detail. However, good candidates will be able to talk about their experiences in depth.

Your aim is to provide a 'fly on the wall' experience for the interviewer so that they can almost imagine themselves having been there when your experience happened.

A worked example of a question and detailed response:

Imagine that an interviewer has asked a candidate the following question: 'Please describe a situation when you have helped a colleague who was in trouble.'

On the face of it, it seems a fairly straightforward question to answer. However, a crafty interviewer could interrupt you at any point and follow up with all sorts of supplementary questions. Look at the following sample candidate's response. You will see certain underlined words and phrases, which indicate points at which the interviewer might want to interrupt to ask for further information.

'There was a time[1] *when James, the sales manager, came to me[2] with a problem[3] about his sales performance[4]. He asked for help, so I tried to be supportive[5] and gave him some* advice[6]. *I also helped him on some site visits[7] to customers. And, over the course of the next few months, he listened to my advice and brought his performance up to satisfactory levels again.'*

The interviewer could potentially ask a variety of additional questions based on the candidate's response so far. For example, the interviewer could ask the following questions:

1. **'You said "there was a time". How recently did this happen?' The candidate responds:**

'This was three years ago, when I'd just moved from the sales department to being the marketing manager. When I left the sales department, they recruited a young sales manager to take over my old role.'

2. **'You said that James came to you. Why did he come to you?'**

'He came to me because we'd already struck up a good working relationship by that point. It was a small company, so I always tried to meet with new colleagues and take them out for a drink and explain to them that I was there if they ever needed any help.'

3. **'And what was the sales manager's problem?'** The candidate explains:

'James wasn't hitting his sales targets. James was a really bright person – but didn't have that much sales experience.'

4. **'What exactly was wrong with his performance?'**

'James had two major targets. His first target was that he had to cold call enough companies every month to set up 5 meetings with prospective clients. His other target was to convert 50 percent of prospective clients into real customers. He was failing on both of them.'

5. *'How were you supportive?'*
The candidate explains:

'James was on the verge of tears and really agitated about his poor performance because he was worried he was going to get fired. The first thing I did was to get him to calm down. I took him out of the office and bought him a coffee and tried to listen to him without judging him.'

6. *'So what were your suggestions?'*
The candidate responds:

'After talking to him and understanding that he was failing to meet both of his targets, my first suggestion was that I might listen in on some of his cold calls. So I spent a few hours one morning listening in on his cold calls. And I discovered that he was telephoning customers without first doing enough research on them. He called them up without knowing anything about their business needs. So I worked with James to think about the sort of facts that he would need to collect before making a call.'

7. *'Tell me a bit more about what you did on these site visits.'*
The candidate responds:

'I also talked James round to letting me attend a couple of sales meetings with him. I went along, observed him and gave him some constructive comments about what he was doing wrong. In particular, he was being a bit too aggressive in trying to get the customer to sign on the dotted line there and then. So I persuaded him to give

customers more thinking time – which resulted in more of
them signing up in the end.'

As you can see, that first question could lead to many other questions that the smart candidate must be ready to answer. Candidates who are exaggerating about their experience could not answer in such detail. However, even honest candidates can get flustered if they have not done some preparation to remind themselves of the situations they have experienced.

GIVING GREAT ANSWERS TO COMPETENCY-BASED QUESTIONS

Now that you understand the sort of questions that an interviewer could ask you, you should recognise the need to prepare your responses in some detail before an interview. In order to equip yourself to respond well to any competency-based questions, you should:

1. Look at the job advert (and job description if you have one). Write down the *dozen* key skills and qualities (i.e. competencies) you think they need for the job. Some of the key skills and qualities may be listed in the advert itself, so look out for phrases such as 'working to deadline', 'handling customers' and 'solving problems'. However, think also about the general skills that may not be listed but are still likely to be important for this kind of work.
2. Think of examples of situations in which you used each of those skills. Sneaky interviewers often ask for more than one example of a skill. So be prepared to answer multiple questions about the same competency. For example, after asking, 'Tell me about a time you had to deal with a difficult problem' the interviewers may listen to your response and then ask, 'Could you tell me about a different problem as well please?'

3. Write your answers down at least in bullet point form. Because interviewers could potentially ask you quite complex questions, it is worth having some notes to help you as you rehearse your answers (see Chapter 3 for more about rehearsing).
4. Finally, think about the follow-on questions that the interviewer might ask you. Look at the worked example above to think about – and how would you answer each one of those supplementary questions.

> *Be sure to answer in the past tense about what you did or what happened. Look out for slippage into the present tense, e.g. statements such as 'I generally try to...' or 'my style is to...'*

Emphasising your role

Use the CAR acronym to create examples that show off the actions you took and the results you achieved:

- **Challenge** – explain in only two or three sentences the situation you faced. Many candidates make the mistake of providing too much background about the problem or opportunity that they had to tackle.
- **Actions** – talk mostly in the first person singular about the actions and steps you took to resolve the situation. So say 'I did...' and 'I decided...' rather than 'we did...' or 'we decided...' At work, we are often taught to talk about 'we' (you may even have been told 'there is no "I" in the word "team" ') but remember that your team is not being interviewed – *you* are.
- **Result** – finish your example with no more than a couple of sentences to summarise the results you achieved, e.g. you fixed

the system malfunction, you resolved the customer's complaint, you helped your colleague to resolve their problem, and so on.

Remember not to spend too long talking about the context to the situation. The important bit is to focus on the actions you took!

Once you have created your CAR examples, you can actually use these to respond to many other questions. For instance, if an interviewer asks you about your strengths, you could list two or three of your strengths and then give a CAR example of one of your strengths. Or if an interviewer asks you a hypothetical question about problems you might face or people with whom you may have to work, you could answer the hypothetical question briefly but then give a real example of how you actually dealt with the similar situation.

Using action words in your examples

Interviewers want to understand that you took actions that delivered results. They don't want to hear that a situation resolved itself without your help! Make sure that you demonstrate your role by describing your actions using positive, action-oriented verbs such as:

Analysed	Created	Interpreted	Produced
Arranged	Established	Mediated	Researched
Asked	Decided	Led	Purchased
Assembled	Discussed	Listened (to)	Repaired
Built	Evaluated	Modified	Reviewed
Calculated	Identified	Motivated	Selected

Communicated	Implemented	Negotiated	Supervised
Compared	Initiated	Organised	Taught
Compiled	Inspected	Persuaded	Tested
Constructed	Inspired (others) to	Planned	

ANSWERING QUESTIONS ABOUT YOUR ACHIEVEMENTS USING THE COMPETENCY-BASED METHOD

Employers want to hire candidates who are self-motivated and driven to succeed. But they also want candidates who can achieve results and make a difference.

'What is your greatest achievement?'

Try to keep your response specific to the job. While you may justly be proud of your family or other achievements outside of work, what will impress the interviewers most is if you talk about work-related achievements such as:

- Increased profit.
- Reduced costs.
- Enhanced productivity.
- Improvements in efficiency.
- Enhanced customer or client satisfaction.
- Improved relationships with suppliers or other stakeholders.
- More effective procedures and processes.
- Improved morale of colleagues.

'I was proudest of the time that I assembled a committee to examine how we deal with patients at the surgery. We identified that many patients were waiting longer than necessary to get appointments because our administrators were processing the paperwork manually. After inviting

colleagues from the IT and admin departments, we made a recommendation to the trustees that we should put in a new computer system. We delivered the system on time and on budget, with the result that we cut waiting times from 18 days to ten days.'

'At the school where I currently work, we didn't have enough money to buy the latest edition of a certain science textbook. However, I took it upon myself to research different options. I contacted several different suppliers and asked them for their prices. Of course they were reluctant to give discounts but I negotiated hard and got a saving of over 15 percent on what we had been spending in the past. So by spending the same amount of money, we managed to get 120 copies of the new textbook effectively for free.'

Remember that an interviewer could possibly ask you further questions such as:

- 'Why is it your biggest achievement?'
- 'Who first identified the problem or situation?'
- 'What was your specific role on the team – as opposed to what your colleagues did?'
- 'What problems or obstacles did you experience along the way? And how did you resolve these?'
- 'What did you learn from this experience?'

'If your greatest achievement happened three years ago, why have you not achieved anything else since then?'

Ideally, you would avoid the interviewers asking you this question by choosing examples that you experienced within the last year or so. However, if you do get this question, avoid letting it throw you. Parry the question by saying:

'That was an achievement that I was especially proud of, but I have accomplished other things since then. For example...'

'What is your second/third/etcetera greatest achievement?'

Be ready to talk about a number of different achievements. Most candidates will have thought about their main achievement – but only the best candidates will be ready to talk about more than one achievement. This is your opportunity to shine!

Take the time to list at least ten work-related achievements. You will never be asked to list ten achievements in one question – but you may be able to use some of your lesser achievements in answer to other questions.

'What is the greatest challenge you have faced and how did you respond to it?'

The interviewer is trying to see how you cope with adversity. Again, steer clear of personal challenges – such as balancing childcare against work commitments or a personal tragedy such as bereavement. While these may have helped to mould you into the person that you are, remember that the interviewer is looking for someone who can overcome the sort of challenges that you would face in the workplace.

In answering this question, think back to an occasion when you were faced with a work problem that at first seemed insurmountable. When talking about how you tackled the problem and triumphed, try to emphasise your personal contribution as opposed to what the rest of the team did.

*'About a year ago, we had too many bookings at the hotel.
It turned out that one of the new customer services people
had overbooked lots of the rooms. So we literally had
dozens of guests arriving with nowhere to stay. Quite a
few of my colleagues were panicking but I arranged with
a couple of local hotels to put the guests up and negotiated
good prices with them so we weren't paying over the odds.
I also invited all of the guests who had to stay in other
hotels to come back to our hotel for free breakfasts so that
they remembered how good our hotel was. As a result of
my actions, we still exceeded our customer satisfaction
targets on our quarterly customer survey.'*

'Tell us about a time you planned and organised a big project'

A good plan is of no use if it does not come off or you end up
dramatically overspending – so employers look for organising
skills as well as being able to implement it on time and within an
agreed budget.

*'The head teacher at my school suggested putting on a
play for the parents and I volunteered to head up the
committee in charge of it. I asked for other teachers to
join me and we discussed who should do what. I made
sure that we made a comprehensive list of everything
that needed doing so nothing could fall between the
cracks. I made sure that we met every week to discuss
progress on issues such as inviting all of the parents
and getting the children involved in everything from
performing in the play to designing the set and scenery
for it. I put in probably a dozen extra hours a week on
top of my normal teaching workload to pull off the play.
We had lots of comments from very delighted parents on
opening night and for several months to come!'*

Remember to prepare for supplementary questions such as:

- 'How did you measure progress along the way?'
- 'Did progress slip against the plan at any point? If so, what did you do to get it back on track again?'
- 'What were the biggest obstacles that you faced along the way? How did you tackle these?'
- 'What did you learn from the experience? What would you do differently next time?'

'Can you talk about a time you persisted in the face of adversity?'

Employers want to hire people who won't give up the moment they come across a minor obstacle. Try to pick an example to share with an interviewer of how you kept your motivation up and kept working until you achieved your goals.

'We had a problem because our creative team wasn't talking with the sales team. So the creative team would create stuff that the sales team couldn't sell. I suggested that we run a workshop to get the creative and sales people together but they didn't want to. I invited both the sales manager and the creative manager to talk to each other and they were a bit reluctant at first, but I kept hammering my point home until they agreed for the three of us to sit down together. At first they couldn't see the benefit of having a workshop for their teams. But we kept talking about it and I arranged two more meetings for the two managers and myself to discuss it. Eventually, I persuaded them about the benefits of the workshop and we set it up.'

'Give me an example of a setback and how you dealt with it'

Again, keep your response focused on the workplace – avoid talking about setbacks such as the breakdown of a significant relationship in your life or failure to achieve a personal goal.

Given that this is a negatively phrased question, the way to respond well is to talk about an occasion when your efforts would have succeeded – were it not for unforeseen circumstances that were completely out of your control.

'I applied for an internal promotion about a year ago. I didn't get the job so I asked for feedback on what I'd done wrong. The interview panel told me that I didn't have enough experience of negotiating deals with our bigger clients. So I approached my boss and asked if I could get more involved in client negotiations. At first I only shadowed him and observed, but then I started to get involved. And I kept asking my boss for feedback and coaching to improve my negotiation skills. Six months later, when the same job came up internally, I applied for it and got the job.'

'Describe a mistake that you made at work and what you did after you identified the mistake'

Everyone makes mistakes – so if you claim never to have made a mistake, the interviewer will just think that you are being defensive. However, don't spend too long spelling out the mistake when the interviewer is most interested in the action you took to rectify it. Try also to highlight what you learned from the experience.

'I worked in the IT support department for a small company. A couple of the team had been sick so I got some temporary staff in. I asked one of the temps to install new virus protection software on all of the company's laptops. It wasn't until about a month later that I discovered that he hadn't finished the job. A virus that stopped everyone from printing affected about 30 of the laptops. So I had to go around each person's laptop, removing the virus and installing the protection software on it. It took me about two hours to do each one and I worked until past midnight for four days in a row to get it all done. I don't blame the temp – it was my fault I hadn't checked that he'd had time to complete the installation. But I learned the hard way not to assume work has been completed without checking it personally.'

'Can you provide me an example of how you have demonstrated initiative?'

This is an opportunity for you to talk about an activity or project that you started on your own – without prompting or being told to do so by someone else.

'The charity I worked for used to run almost entirely on donations from the public collected by our volunteers rattling collecting tins, but donations were falling by over 10 percent per year. We identified that it would only be two years before we would be forced to close the animal shelter. My colleagues saw this as simply inevitable, but I was determined not to let it happen. So I just picked up the local telephone directory and spent two weeks phoning up local businesses to try to get their support. I called over 300 companies and got turned down by 99

percent of them. But I managed to persuade nine local businesses to donate £11,000 in return for allowing them to put our logo on their corporate Christmas cards. As such, we identified that the charity does have a future – but that we need to collect from corporate sponsors in the future rather than the general public.'

'Can you give me an example of how you have developed yourself?'

In answering this question, be sure to demonstrate that you took it upon yourself to develop your skills and know-how. Being forced by your boss to go on a course because you were failing to perform well in your job does not make for a great example!

'In order to get better at my job, I realised that I needed to learn more about our front-line operations. It's all very well commissioning market research about what our customers want, but I decided that there was no substitute for actually speaking to some of our customers myself. So I asked if I could visit several of our call centres for a couple of days a month. I listened in on both inbound and outbound phonecalls with customers to get a better sense of what they do and don't like about our business. Getting that customer perspective has really helped me to develop new services we can offer our customers.'

'Tell me about a time you learnt a new way of working at work'

Organisations are continuously on the lookout for new, better ways of working. You've probably heard of terms such as:

- Globalisation
- Outsourcing
- Offshoring

- Business process improvement
- Restructuring
- Reorganisation
- Change programme

Your aim in talking about change is not just to show that you are able to cope with change (as opposed to being one of the curmudgeons who fear change). Be sure to demonstrate that you not only tolerate change but actively embrace it.

'Our department recently outsourced our accounts process. Rather than being able to just walk down the corridor to sort out queries, the biggest change was that we now send documents through to an accounts centre in India. There have been lots of difficulties and a lot of my colleagues have felt really frustrated. But I see this as a necessary part of our future. It's a new way for us to do business more cost effectively so I have been spending a lot of time supporting my colleagues and encouraging them to be more patient with the accounts centre as they learn the job.'

HANDLING COMPETENCY-BASED QUESTIONS ABOUT YOUR PEOPLE SKILLS

Almost all employers are interested in whether you can get on with other people and work effectively with them. They want to explore the extent to which you can influence, persuade, or motivate others to achieve results on your behalf.

'Who is the most difficult person you have worked with and what did you do about them?'

This question is trying to determine how you deal with conflict. Try to give an example that illustrates a difference of opinion or misunderstanding that you resolved through calm discussion.

'When I was working as a senior account executive for this large advertising firm, we had quite a difficult office manager. He was generally an asset to the company, but could at times be quite snappy when he was very busy. On one occasion, one of the junior members of my team came to me in tears. She had asked him for help to prepare a presentation for a client but he had been unhelpful and even shouted and called her some unpleasant names. So I asked the office manager to come out for lunch with me and I gave him some tough feedback on how forthright he could get when he was under pressure. However, I emphasised that he was a very valuable member of our team and didn't want to lose him. At first he was quite defensive and refused to listen. But I gave him more specific examples of when he had been quite brutal and he came to acknowledge the problem. Very quickly after that, we all saw a change in his behaviour in terms of being more considerate.'

Avoid giving an example in which you lost your temper or even felt angry and emotional.

Whatever your response, remember that (as with all competency-based questions), you must be ready to talk further about what you said or did. Other questions that the interviewer might use to probe further your style of dealing with difficult people include:

- 'When you confronted this person, could you describe in more detail exactly what you said?'
- 'What were your options in trying to change this person's mind?'

'Can you tell me about a team you were proud to have been a part of?'

In talking about a team you were a part of, make sure you can demonstrate how you *actively contributed* to the success of the team.

'When I started work at the law library, I noticed that the other librarians tended to be quite solitary. They would go off on their lunch breaks and be quite stubborn about changing their break times and helping each other out. So I suggested that we spend time socialising together outside of work. I came up with the idea of booking out one Friday every month when we would all go out together as a team. I suggested that a few of us every month should come up with an idea for somewhere different to go and organise a trip for us all. Over the course of several months, everyone started to get on much better and we all noticed that people were willing to be much more flexible in helping each other out.'

'Tell me about a time you influenced someone or changed their mind'

Choose an example of a peer, rather than a subordinate, that you have influenced. Claiming to have changed the mind of someone that you manage does not really count – as they really have little choice but to listen to you if you are their boss.

Or, if you have ever convinced a customer to buy from you or negotiated a better deal with a supplier – you could use that as your example of having influenced someone.

When constructing your response, remember that there are many different ways of changing a person's mind. Some people, for example, can be convinced by a logical argument backed by facts and figures. Others, however, may not respect what the facts say – they may need to be influenced by praise and compliments.

'When I was a customer service manager for an overnight delivery company, we were invited to pitch for the contract to handle all of the deliveries for a large business. We put together a good proposal but were told by the customer that we weren't the cheapest. We couldn't drop our price any further because it would have been unprofitable for us, so I tried to persuade the customer that we would be a lower risk than our cheaper competitors. I invited him to see how our distribution centre worked and introduced him to the supervisors and staff. In the end, he liked what he saw and decided that our higher prices would ensure fewer breakages – so he signed a two-year contract with us.'

'Give me an example of a time you successfully sold a product or service'

This is the kind of question that is only relevant to candidates that would be expected to do any significant amount of selling or business development. As with any other competency-based question, think about how the challenge arose but spend most of your time describing the actions that *you* took.

Remember that you are being interviewed as an individual for the job, so speak in the first person singular as opposed to the first person plural. Yes, there may have been a team involved in winning the customer, but tell the interviewer about your specific contribution – what 'I' did as opposed to what 'we' did.

If you are a sales person (or have to sell as part of your role), you might also want to think about related questions including:

- 'Tell me about the last client pitch you made. How did you prepare and how did it go?'
- 'Give me an example of a time you won a new customer.'
- 'Talk me through how you grew an existing customer account.'

'Give me an example of how you have gained buy-in from another person or persons'

This question is no different to being asked to give an example of how you have persuaded someone that your ideas were right. Don't let yourself be put off by the concept of 'buy-in', which is simply organisational jargon for 'acceptance'.

'When have you managed to persuade someone more senior than you to change their mind?'

Another variation of the basic question on how you have changed someone's mind. However, it is worth thinking about an occasion when you might have convinced someone more senior than yourself. Trying to influence upwards requires greater political sensitivity than influencing a peer – so try to reflect this in your response.

'Talk me through an occasion when you had to say "no" to someone'

An interviewer may also ask: 'When was the last time you had to be assertive?' The key in answering this question is to show that you can stand up for what you believe is right, but without being pushy or at all aggressive.

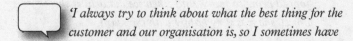

'I always try to think about what the best thing for the customer and our organisation is, so I sometimes have *said "no" in the past. For example, my boss recently had a call from a customer demanding that someone should visit their office to sort out a problem. My boss told me that I had to drop whatever else I was doing to go to that customer. But with a little digging I realised that the problem could be sorted out over the phone and didn't actually require a personal visit, so I explained that sensitively to my boss, who was fine about my solution.'*

'Tell me about the most demanding customer/client situation you have faced and how you dealt with it'

Customer service or client focus is often an important competency. If you don't have external customers or clients, think about who your internal customers are.

This question is really a variation of the 'tell me about a difficult person' question. Just make sure that your response includes a happy ending about how you resolved the situation to the satisfaction of both the customer but also your organisation.

'I had a client who was very demanding. Even when we had agreed certain deadlines for our team to deliver the work, she would be on the telephone a couple of times a day to chase us and check up on us. Some of my colleagues were starting to feel the pressure and were starting to get a bit agitated and irritable. I could see what was happening so I set up a meeting with the client and told her very politely and very gently about the impact her chasing was having on us. She hadn't appreciated that she was actually stopping us from working more effectively. To cut a long story short, she stopped being so picky. And when we did deliver the project, she was very happy with the result.'

HANDLING QUESTIONS ABOUT DECISIONS AND PROBLEM-SOLVING

Problems crop up in work every day of our working lives. To show that you are a good candidate, you need to be able to demonstrate to a prospective employer that you gave good analytical and problem-solving skills.

'Tell me about a difficult problem and how you tackled it'

Don't spend too much time describing the problem. Instead, talk about how you analysed the situation and describe the steps you took to tackle the problem.

'The MD had issued instructions that each of our branches had to cut costs by 18 percent. I was the branch manager at the time. Everyone who worked for me knew that this probably meant redundancies. However, I gathered the team together and ran a big brainstorming session, throwing dozens of ideas onto flip charts. One of the suggestions was that we could partition off part of the branch and sub-let the space to another company. I thought it was a good idea, so I set up a project team to explore how it would work. I then called in contractors to put up a dividing wall, refurbish the space and fill it with new office furniture and equipment. Then we advertised in the local press and found a company to take the space. We managed to reduce our costs by 21 percent, and avoided any redundancies.'

Remember to emphasise your role by talking in the first person singular – 'I did…' or 'I said' or 'I invited' and so on.

'Describe a time when you had a difficult decision to make'

Rather than talking about difficult personal decisions you may have had (e.g. to move house, or split up from a partner), you should try to talk about a decision that ultimately benefited your employer.

This is a question with a couple of parts. In order to show an interviewer that you can make good decisions, an ideal answer would include at least some of the following steps:

■ Gathering further information to understand the situation properly to avoid jumping to conclusions too quickly.
■ Involving other people to check that your information was correct or seeking their participation to get ideas on how to tackle the problem.
■ Identifying possible options for tackling the problem and/or weighing up the pros and cons of each option.

'We had a lot of work on and a client asked us to do some further work for us. We were already very stretched so I didn't know if we could handle it. I went and met the client, listened to their situation, and went back to the office to think through whether we could do it. I calculated the number of days it would take to do the project and discovered that we simply couldn't do it. I considered a number of options including hiring someone in to help with the work, but at the end of the day I decided that the best thing for the long-term relationship with the client was to apologise and say that we couldn't do the work. If we had taken on the work, we would have done it poorly and damaged the relationship, and I know that the client respected us for not taking on the project.'

'Describe a situation in which you made a bad decision'

This question may be asked as a follow-up after you have given a good response to the preceding question on a difficult decision that you made. The interviewer is trying to probe a decision that did not go to plan.

A good answer might admit that the *outcome* of the decision was wrong – but that there was nothing wrong with the way in which you came to your decision. Perhaps you were under severe time pressure and were faced with either making a quick decision or losing a significant opportunity altogether. Or maybe you were forced to take a decision where there was no clear right or wrong.

'This was two years ago, when our company had been busy setting up overseas offices in Europe and we had neglected to plan our Christmas party. It was coming up to the end of November and we hadn't decided on a venue. I volunteered to research a shortlist of restaurants or hotels that could accommodate 70 employees and their partners. I phoned about 40 venues and I found two hotels that could take us at such short notice. Unfortunately, there simply wasn't time to consult everyone else in the company, so I went for a quick look around the two venues and chose one, sorted out the menu, and booked a local DJ. It wasn't our best Christmas party, but at least we had one, so I stand by my decision because it was the best that I could find at such short notice.'

Be ready for the obvious follow-up question: 'What did you learn from your decision – and what would you do differently next time?'

'Give me an example of when you've had to be creative'

This is your opportunity to impress the interviewer with your blue-sky, out-of-the-box thinking.

'Our departmental budget was slashed by 17 percent last year, so we had a lot less money to spend but we still had to meet the same targets. So I suggested that we run a brainstorming session to come up with new ideas. I persuaded human resources to buy in some pizza and drinks one Thursday evening and I stood at a flip chart prompting people, persuading them to contribute, and noting down all of the wacky ideas that people could think of to still do a great job with less money. We came up with some really good ideas and I personally came up with the idea of selling off our old computers to a local college, which raised nearly £2,000.'

IN SUMMARY...

- Examine the job advert (and job description if you have one) to identify the skills or competencies that the interviewer is likely to ask you about.
- Prepare at least two examples of situations in which you demonstrated each competency.
- Make sure you can explain the actions you took – remember you are there to sell yourself and not the rest of your team.
- Be prepared to talk in a lot more detail about each situation if the interviewer wants more detail.

Chapter 7

HANDLING WEIRD, WONDERFUL AND WRONGFUL QUESTIONS

In this chapter …
- **Telling the interviewers what they want to hear**
- **Responding positively to negative questions**
- **How to open up closed questions**
- **Dealing with illegal questions with finesse**

Skilled interviewers know that they put candidates at their ease and get them to talk about how they have used their skills and experience in the past. Unfortunately, many interviewers have never been trained and, because they don't know any better, may end up asking up some fairly crazy questions!

HANDLING QUESTIONS DESIGNED TO EXPLORE HOW YOU THINK

Some questions can't possibly tell the interviewer anything about your ability to do the job – but obviously the interviewer thinks that it is a good question. So you have no choice really but to have a shot at responding briefly to the question, then trying to turn the question to your advantage to show off some skill.

'What was the last book you read?'

Few interviewers will expect you to have read a business book. Just be ready to discuss the plot or contents of a book that you have read. Ideally, the book should have improved you in at least some small way. If you can, try to show how the book has benefits for your working life.

'I read a book that talks about the plight of the servant classes in turn-of-the-century China. It's a very humbling description of the effects of poverty and injustice.'

 'I'm reading a book at the moment on emotional intelligence, which is about how people can build more successful relationships with other people. I'm learning quite a lot about understanding other people's perspectives and improving my listening skills with colleagues.'

✓ *Don't be caught lying – if you are going to say that you have read a key business book, then be ready to answer technical questions about the content of the book.*

'Who in your life has inspired you?'

As with many of these questions, the person you name is perhaps less important than the reasons you give for identifying that person.

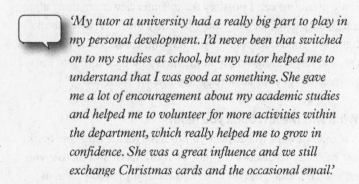 *'My tutor at university had a really big part to play in my personal development. I'd never been that switched on to my studies at school, but my tutor helped me to understand that I was good at something. She gave me a lot of encouragement about my academic studies and helped me to volunteer for more activities within the department, which really helped me to grow in confidence. She was a great influence and we still exchange Christmas cards and the occasional email.'*

'What was the last news story that caught your eye?'

Interviewers sometimes like to know that candidates keep up-to-date with current affairs. Whatever story you choose to mention, try to relate it back to the job you are being interviewed for.

'I was just reading about the big banking merger which will create a new financial services giant with over 140,000 employees. I can imagine that will be a big opportunity for an IT contracting business such as yours.'

Make it a habit to buy a quality newspaper (or read up on the newspaper's website) and scan the top handful of stories on the day of any interview.

'What was the last film you saw?'

It does not matter what the last film you saw was. Just be prepared to talk briefly about the plot and why you saw it.

'I saw Action Movie 4, *which was a big budget adventure movie. I watch all sorts of things from independent French films to romantic comedies, but on this occasion I wanted something escapist to watch.'*

'See this pencil I'm holding? Sell it to me'

This is a common question – and rarely asked of salespeople. You could be asked to sell just about anything that the interviewer has within reach – from a lamp to the chairs you are both sitting on. The interviewer is trying to put you on the spot, testing how you respond to the sort of unexpected pressures that can crop up at work as well as your ability to communicate and sell ideas.

Think of the interviewer as a potential customer for the object that you are being asked to sell, and complete the following three steps:

1. Ask the interviewer about his or her needs and exposure to objects of this sort. For example, if you were selling a chair: 'How would you rate the chairs around your house or in the office? Do you need to sit at a desk for many hours of the day?'
2. Talk about key *features* of the object. For example, a chair may be comfortable. A pen may be filled with red ink.
3. Discuss some of the key *benefits* of the object. A comfortable chair could help the interviewer to work for longer without getting backache. A red ink pen could help him to correct documents more easily without confusing the corrections with the original text.

'If you were an animal, what would you be?'

The interviewer has probably read a 'pop psychology' book claiming that candidates can be rated based on the type of animal they would describe themselves as. This is a silly question as there is no link between job performance and types of animal.

Unfortunately, you need to play along with this amateur Freud. Select a suitably noble animal such as a lion, eagle, wolf, etc. and go on to relate how its characteristics relate to your ability to do the job. Resist the temptation to choose an animal with comical or sinister qualities such as a sloth or a snake.

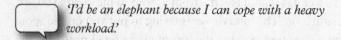

'I'd be an elephant because I can cope with a heavy workload.'

'I'd be a Labrador because I pick up skills quickly and I'm good around other people.'

There are endless variations on this question. I have also heard an interviewer ask: 'If you were a type of vehicle, what would you be?' Again, think about certain cars that are known for their reliability, or speed, etc.

'Tell me a story'

Ideally, you should tell a story about your career, including examples of the skills that the interviewer is looking for. Perhaps first ask, 'Can I tell you the story of my career?'

However, if the interviewer insists that you tell a story about something outside of work, try to tell a story about something that you have achieved – whether it is learning a musical instrument or designing an extension for your house.

 'I decided five years ago that I was getting a bit out of shape so I decided to get fit. I joined a local gym and started an exercise programme. I was very unfit to begin with and I used to ache after coming back from my routines, but I was determined to stick with it. I made sure that I'd go at least once every weekend and once during the week and possibly twice if I could manage it. After about six months, I'd lost a bit of weight and discovered that I had a lot more energy. I've kept up the exercising ever since.'

 Alternatively, try to tell the interviewer the story of how you triumphed against adversity in some way, perhaps while you were growing up. Make sure the story has a happy ending!

'If you could meet anyone living or dead, who would it be and why?'

Pick someone who has characteristics or skills that would be desirable in the job you are applying for – such as a notable business leader. However, resist citing the really well known business gurus such as Tom Peters or Warren Bennis – as that could make you sound clichéd. Politicians can also be risky choices if you do not know the political leanings of your interviewer. Also steer clear of poets, humanitarians, or artists – unless you can argue that they have traits that you would use for this particular job.

'I would like to meet Sir Peter Alexander, who was the chief executive of Matazar, the European retailer. The firm grew from five shops to 80 shops and saw sales grow by over 1,000 percent in six years. I'd love to pick his brains about his vision for the retail industry.'

'Who do you admire and why?'

I have said it before, but I shall say it again: Think about the skills or competencies that the interviewing organisation is looking for. Perhaps you could talk about a tutor or previous boss who was a good role model for one of those skills. Giving an example of a manager that you have worked for will also give the interviewer the impression that you are respectful of those who are senior to you.

'My previous manager was a really good role model. She was on the fast track to partnership at the firm, but almost invariably managed to squeeze her workload into a 9am to 6pm day. She was very focused on her work during the day, which allowed her to have a good work-life balance too. I'd like to believe I've learnt some of her

tricks for managing her workload and getting more done during the day.'

'What kind of manager would you like to work for?'

Your answer depends on what you know about the organisation. So make sure you do some research on how you are likely to be managed. For example, if you think that the organisation is driven by strict rules and procedures, you might say:

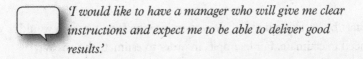

'I would like to have a manager who will give me clear instructions and expect me to be able to deliver good results.'

If the organisation is known for its creativity and giving employees a great deal of autonomy, a candidate might say:

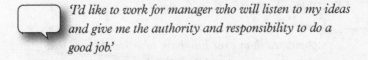

'I'd like to work for manager who will listen to my ideas and give me the authority and responsibility to do a good job.'

'How many cars are there in Australia?'

Management consultancies and investment banks, in particular, like to ask questions that may require you to 'guesstimate' an answer. Typical questions might ask you to estimate the size of a market, for example: 'How many mobile phones are there in China?' or 'How many litres of orange juice are consumed in France each year?'

On the face of it, these would seem impossible to answer, as you are not going to have the facts to hand. However, the interviewer is actually interested in two key skills:

1. Your capacity to make estimates, apply rules of thumb, and

extrapolate from information that you do possess when no definitive data is available.

2. How quickly you can make mental calculations.

The interviewer is not expecting you to have the actual answers. They are more interested in hearing your thought processes on tackling the question. So one critical tip (which the interviewers often forget to mention) is to talk aloud as you work out the answer to the problem.

Start by breaking down the question into the facts that you would need to estimate. For example, in order to estimate the answer, you need to know how many people are in Australia. Then you would need to figure out the ratio of people to cars in the country. A candidate's answer might go along the lines of the following:

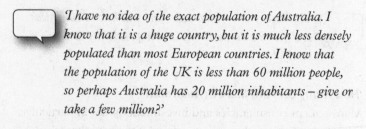

'I have no idea of the exact population of Australia. I know that it is a huge country, but it is much less densely populated than most European countries. I know that the population of the UK is less than 60 million people, so perhaps Australia has 20 million inhabitants – give or take a few million?'

'Now, not everyone has a car. People may live in family units – so even though there may be 20 million people living in Australia, we probably only have about 7 million households, because on average maybe three people live in each household. Not every household has a car though, so let's say that only one in two households has a car. Obviously, some households have more than one car – but there are lots of people who travel only on public transport. So of the 7 million households, I'd say there were about 3.5 million cars in Australia.'

Now, your estimates may have a significant margin of error attached to them. But as long as they are sensible and not completely ridiculous – you can demonstrate your ability to break a problem down and make rapid mental calculations.

'Why are supermarket own-brand cans of baked beans cheaper than the leading make of branded baked beans?'

No technical knowledge about food production is actually needed to answer the question as this question is trying to ascertain the candidate's ability to make sensible assumptions and to break down an initially complicated-seeming problem.

In such a situation, the interviewer is looking for your ability to:

■ Apply logic to break a complex problem into a number of more easily solved component problems.
■ Gather and analyse information.
■ Make suggestions while thinking on your feet.

> *If the question involves multiple points and sub-questions, ask whether the interviewer would mind you jotting down some of the key points on a sheet of paper to act as a reminder.*

A candidate's answer might go as follows:

> *'Well, I assume that own-brand baked beans are cheaper because they cost less to produce. So why don't we break down the cost of different cans of beans into their constituent parts?'*

> *'Thinking about the constituent parts, there are the basic costs of the beans themselves. Perhaps the branded*

*company can buy beans in more cheaply, because they
buy in bigger quantities and can get them in bulk. The
branded beans company would also probably be able to
buy in tin cans more cheaply, again because they buy in
greater quantities. However, those two facts would suggest
that the branded beans should be cheaper – so that's not
the answer.'*

*'Another part of the cost is the distribution of the
tins of beans – but I can't see why there would be a
significant difference in cost there either. Aha – I've got it.
Supermarkets never advertise their baked beans on the
television, whereas the branded company has to spend
much more on marketing and advertising. So that's why
supermarkets can sell their beans more cheaply.'*

And there is the answer. So remember that succeeding at case
study interviews is about breaking down a problem, and then
making some quick estimates and mental calculations.

**'You are in a room with three light switches, each of which
controls one of three light bulbs in an adjacent room. You must
determine which switch controls which bulb. But I'm afraid you
may only flick two switches and may enter the adjacent room
only once. How would you go about determining which switch
controls which bulb?'**

Some interviewers like to pose riddles, quandaries, or
brainteasers to test candidates' ability to 'think out of the box'.
These are unlikely to have a right or wrong answer – in fact
there may be many possible solutions. The only tip here is to let
your imagination run wild.

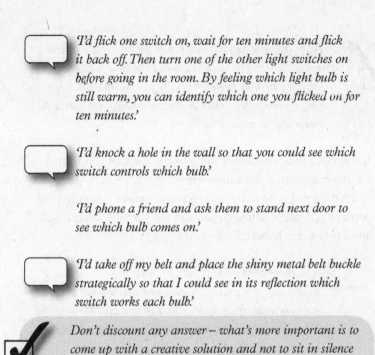

'I'd flick one switch on, wait for ten minutes and flick it back off. Then turn one of the other light switches on before going in the room. By feeling which light bulb is still warm, you can identify which one you flicked on for ten minutes.'

'I'd knock a hole in the wall so that you could see which switch controls which bulb.'

'I'd phone a friend and ask them to stand next door to see which bulb comes on.'

'I'd take off my belt and place the shiny metal belt buckle strategically so that I could see in its reflection which switch works each bulb.'

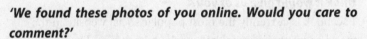

Don't discount any answer – what's more important is to come up with a creative solution and not to sit in silence looking confused.

'We found these photos of you online. Would you care to comment?'

Increasingly, I hear about candidates who've been rejected because of what employers found online about them – despite the candidates having good CVs and otherwise coming over well during the interview. So check what's online about you to make sure this question doesn't catch you out in the middle of an interview.

If you are a member of any social networking websites, be extremely cautious about what you put online about yourself. Be careful what you allow friends to post online about you too.

Type your name into a handful of the big online search engines (currently, Google, Yahoo, Bing and Ask) and check the first ten pages of results you get on each. If you find anything that could be even remotely misconstrued, find a way to remove it.

If you can't remove the offending material about you from the Internet, then at least have a good explanation. So long as you have a response to the question and deliver it calmly (and perhaps self-deprecatingly), you can reassure the interviewers and avoid being knocked off-course.

'Oh, those photos were taken a couple of years ago at a work fancy dress party, so everyone was dressed like that, even our managing director and chairman. Of course I don't usually go around in public wearing only my underwear!'

'If we looked at your Facebook profile, what impression do you think it would give us of you?'

Facebook is currently the most popular social website in the world so it's the one site that employers are most likely to check. In order to be certain that your online window to the world creates only a good impression of you, it's worth checking your privacy settings to ensure that what you make public to the world says only good things about you. If you are in any doubt, ask a friend to scrutinise your profile for you.

In answering the question, be sure to repeat back to the interviewer some of the skills or qualities that are required for the job.

'I think I have a fun side, but I'm also responsible and deeply passionate about my work.'

DEFLECTING NEGATIVE QUESTIONS WITH A POSITIVE APPROACH

In the bad old days of interviewing, quite a few interviewers used to think that giving candidates a hard time and deliberately putting them under stress was a good idea. By doing so, they hope to expose personality flaws in weaker candidates. Luckily, most interviewers know better – although there may still be one or two interviewers who haven't heard that stress interviews are out.

If you are faced with an aggressive interviewer, you must keep your composure. Responding with anger will only escalate the situation. Remember that you want to be offered a job, so you need to hide your irritation. Be calm, take your time, and focus on answering the question.

Some questions start by making a negative statement about you, and invite you to fight your way uphill to impress the interviewer. Because these questions can be convoluted, you should take a few seconds to ensure that you have understood the question properly before responding.

'I don't understand why you think you are the right person for this job'

You might want to ask the interviewer why he or she thinks so: 'Can I ask why you think that?' or 'Could you be a bit more specific, please? What exactly are your doubts?'

Then try to make a short statement about why you think you are the right person for the job:

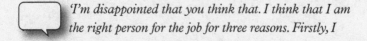 *'I'm disappointed that you think that. I think that I am the right person for the job for three reasons. Firstly, I*

*have a track record of delivering exceptional customer
service, which is something that my last boss will attest
to. Secondly, I've been told by various colleagues that I
have a better understanding of this particular technology
than some of the people who work for the company that
invented the technology. And finally, I'm incredibly
determined and I can give you a couple of examples of
how I've persisted to deliver results for the team.'*

'Why do you think that you are better than the other candidates?'

The question asserts that you think you are better than the other
candidates – and you need to correct that assertion. Use this
question as an opportunity to summarise again what you believe
are your key strengths.

*'I haven't met the other candidates, so I can only talk
about myself. What I hope I have done is to impress you
with my track record of results. In particular, I think I
have three main strengths, which are…'*

'Do you like regular hours and routine working patterns?'

Be sure to tell the interviewer what you think they need to hear.

*Be sure to tailor your response to what you know about
the organisation. Is it the sort of organisation where the
work may be very repetitive and predictable or incredibly
varied?*

*'Yes, I like to get comfortable with a job so that I can do
it well.'*

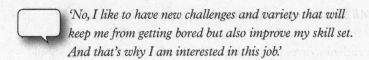

'No, I like to have new challenges and variety that will keep me from getting bored but also improve my skill set. And that's why I am interested in this job.'

'Do you mind paperwork and other bureaucratic practices?'

The interviewer might be trying to hint that the job will involve a lot of administrative work. Good research about the demands of the job will help you to decide on the right answer to give.

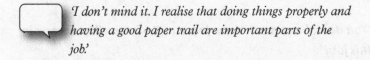

'I don't mind it. I realise that doing things properly and having a good paper trail are important parts of the job.'

'Have you ever broken rules to get a job done?'

Be careful here, as there is a critical difference between breaking a rule once to achieve a benefit to the organisation and breaking rules on multiple occasions because you find rules restrictive.

When answering, explain that you broke a rule only because there was an opportunity or challenge to which you had to react quickly – the organisation would have lost out if you had not broken the rules.

'I have broken the rules – but only because the rule was stopping me from achieving what I knew my boss wanted. I had been asked to get quotes from three companies on the costs of printing a brochure that we needed for the end of the week. I am supposed to get her to sign off on expenditure over £1,000, but she had been called into a meeting. The cheapest quote came in at about £1,200 – but I gave them the go-ahead anyway, because otherwise we would not have had the brochures done by the end of the week.'

'All of us have personality defects – what is yours?'

A personality defect is a very strong term and it would be prudent to avoid admitting to having any. However, you should not try to imply that you are perfect, so go on to talk about one of your minor weaknesses (see pages 90–2).

'I wouldn't say that I have anything as strong as a personality defect. However, I do have areas that I know I could improve on. For example...'

'You don't have much experience of X – how will you cope in this job?'

The 'X' could represent just about any skill. The interviewer may have spotted from your CV that you don't have much experience with a particular system, tool, method of working, software package, etc. that this organisation uses. Your response must reassure the interviewer that you at least have *similar* experience – and that you learn fast.

'I've used several other similar design programmes. When I first joined my current company, I hadn't had any experience of the Design 200 software but I found that it was sufficiently similar to other packages that I was able to get up to speed with it very quickly. I had to work a bit harder and for slightly longer hours than the rest of the team for a few weeks, but the fact that I'd not used the programme before certainly didn't impact upon my work performance.'

'Do you take work home with you in the evenings or at weekends?'

A question that tries to trap you into admitting that you are ineffective during the day and need to catch up in the evenings and at weekends.

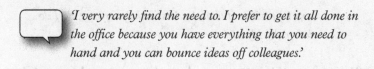

'I very rarely find the need to. I prefer to get it all done in the office because you have everything that you need to hand and you can bounce ideas off colleagues.'

'Why did you not achieve more in your last job?'

The interviewer may be trying to provoke you into reacting emotionally. Try to talk about what you did achieve rather than focusing on what you did not achieve.

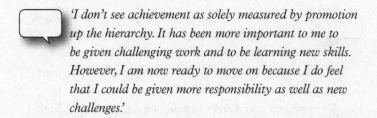

'I don't see achievement as solely measured by promotion up the hierarchy. It has been more important to me to be given challenging work and to be learning new skills. However, I am now ready to move on because I do feel that I could be given more responsibility as well as new challenges.'

'Quite frankly, I don't think you have enough experience of...'

If the interviewer expresses a concern about a skill or experience that you do actually have (but he or she just does not know about), you should give an example to make it clear to the interviewer that you do possess it.

However, if you do not have the required skill or experience, you would need to emphasise your willingness and ability to learn. Give an example of a related skill that you picked up very quickly.

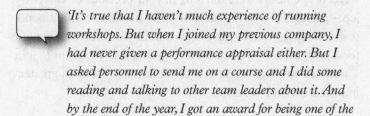

'It's true that I haven't much experience of running workshops. But when I joined my previous company, I had never given a performance appraisal either. But I asked personnel to send me on a course and I did some reading and talking to other team leaders about it. And by the end of the year, I got an award for being one of the

*top 10 percent of team leaders in the company. So I do
learn quickly.'*

'How do you think your experience has prepared you to take on more responsibility?'

A good response should talk about the opportunities you have already had in your current or previous jobs to take on more responsibility.

*'I've actually already had some experience of managing
a restaurant. When a shift manager was sometimes
unable to come to work, I was usually the one who
assumed responsibility for the team. So I'd be the point
of contact if customers had any complaints. I'd be the
one who would order in more stock, take the cash bags
to the bank, and lock up the premises last thing at night.
Over the last six months alone, I've probably spent at
least a dozen days taking on the full range of managerial
responsibilities.'*

'Aren't you overqualified (or have too much experience) for this job?'

The employer may be worried that you might get bored
of the job and move on quickly. If you agree that you are
overqualified, you could try explaining that you are looking
for a better work-life balance. There may have been too much
travel or the hours were too long in your previous or current
job – perhaps you have family or other personal commitments
that mean you want to have some stability in your working life
for a few years. Or you could try arguing that you want to join
a smaller company where you can feel that you have a greater
impact on what goes on.

Whatever you say, make sure you can state your case convincingly to explain how you will still be committed to the job – that you're not burnt out and looking for an opportunity to slacken off entirely.

'I realise on paper that this may look like a step down from being a manager to one of the team. But I've come to the conclusion that I prefer the day-to-day business of graphic design to having to manage a team. I get much more enjoyment out of doing it than managing others who are doing it – and that's why I'm currently looking for jobs only as a designer rather than a design manager.'

'Have you ever been fired?'

The best answer would be to say, 'no'. However, if you cannot, then you will need to have good reasons why it happened. Finish by reassuring the interviewer that it was a one-time situation that will never again occur.

'I had a major difference of opinion with my boss. I felt that some of his practices were misleading. For example, when customers rang in with complaints, he encouraged us to lie to cover up why we hadn't got the right products to them on time. We clashed on quite a few occasions and eventually my boss asked me to leave. However, I've worked for four other bosses in my career so far and I could ask any of those other bosses for a reference and they would tell you how good I am in a team.'

'I joined the company because I thought I would be working on lots of big, strategic projects. However, when I joined, I discovered that the job actually involved

a lot of dealing with the detail and administration. I really should have quit but unfortunately I let it affect my motivation. As a consequence, I was asked to leave. However, I learnt my lesson and now am much more careful to understand the demands of the jobs I apply for. This job, for instance, is exactly the kind of job that would play to my strengths because it would allow me to concentrate on those broad, big picture issues.'

'What keeps you up at night?'

In reality, most people have a combination of both personal and professional worries. However, you may want to downplay the extent to which you agonise over work-related issues:

'I don't think anything keeps me up at night, to be honest. I have concerns, obviously – but for the most part I feel that I am in control of my life. At work, I want to do a good job and feel that people respect me for my work. But I wouldn't say that these trouble me overly.'

'How would you rate me as an interviewer?'

It would be dangerous to express your honest opinion if the interviewer is boring you or asking the wrong sort of questions! Be diplomatic and constructive if you want to make any small criticisms.

'I'd rate you as a good interviewer because you've asked me some fairly challenging questions that have made me work hard and have to really think about the answers. But at the same time you have also given me a chance to talk about my skills and experience. So yes, all round it's been a good performance on your part.'

'What do you not want me to ask you?'

Interviewers are unlikely to ask you this precise question but take a moment right now to think about the question or questions that you might be hoping not to be asked by an interviewer.

For example, perhaps you suffered a period of ill health and are hoping that the topic won't come up. Maybe you didn't get on with your last boss and are dreading questions about that work relationship. Or you had been running your own small business which failed and now you have to seek employment again.

The point here is to think ahead of how you might respond to such questions. Think of an answer that allows you to respond to the question briefly but then move quickly on to a more positive topic.

'Yes, I experienced a period of depression and took some time away from work to get better. However, I am fully recovered now and really excited by the massive growth of the industry. I think I can make a huge contribution because I faced a similar situation in one of my previous roles. I can tell you about that if you like.'

Remember to spend as little time as possible talking about the negative aspects of your situation. Move as quickly as you can on to more positive topics.

OPENING UP CLOSED QUESTIONS

Technically, you could get away with answering only 'yes' or 'no' to closed questions. However, you will give the interviewer a much clearer picture of your skills and fit with the organisation if you continue by giving an example to explain your 'yes' or 'no' answer.

'Do you ever have any doubts about your ability to do the job?'

Insecurity is a deeply unattractive trait in potential employees. Who wants to work with someone who needs constant reassurance? However, be careful not to sound arrogant in your response.

'Of course there are moments when you feel tired and frustrated. But I can honestly say that for 99 percent of the time, I get a real kick out of the variety, the pace, and having challenging deadlines. Keeping busy and learning new things is how I know I'm still alive.'

'Do you regard it as a weakness to lose your temper?'

A 'yes' could imply that no one should ever lose his or her temper. But a 'no' could imply that you lose your temper regularly.

'I can't think of an occasion when I have personally lost my temper at work. However, I recognise that we're all only human – it could happen to me in the future. So I try to be patient and understanding of the reasons why someone else may be angry.'

Consider as an alternative explaining that you sometimes feel frustrated but somehow manage to bite your tongue or otherwise calm yourself to avoid taking it out on people at work.

'When was the last time you felt frustrated at work?'

Try to avoid saying that you feel frustrated by other people. Perhaps talk about how some system or process at work stops you from achieving organisational goals more effectively.

'I don't really get frustrated by much. Although I do sometimes think that if we didn't have to submit all budget applications through head office, we could save a lot of time. Having said that, I appreciate that head office wants to make sure that we are not overspending. But it is slightly frustrating that we can't meet customers' requests a little more quickly.'

However, if an interviewer insists on an example of when you last felt frustrated by another person, give a response that shows you might have felt slightly frustrated, but in no way let it affect your working relationship or your ability to do the job.

'I have a colleague who speaks and laughs incredibly loudly. Sometimes when we're on the telephone with customers, I know that the customer can hear her. I don't want the customer to think that we're being unprofessional so I'm constantly telling my colleague to quieten down – politely, of course. Various colleagues and I have probably mentioned it to her several dozen times, but she soon forgets to be quiet and becomes loud again.'

'Do you mind travelling much?'

If you do mind having to travel, I would recommend that you keep your mouth shut until you have been offered the job and have the opportunity to negotiate exactly how much you will have to travel. But simply answering 'no' is not enough.

'It is part of the job and I am used to it. I find that I can catch up with my reading on trains.'

'One of the reasons I'm looking to join you is because of the prospect of international travel. I want to experience different cultures and learn about the different ways in which business is conducted elsewhere, so I'm really looking forward to travelling quite a bit.'

'Good morning. Would you like a hot drink before we start?'
Not a trick question. If you would like to, then do accept a drink, as you may be talking for a few hours and need to moisten your mouth and throat. But rather than have your interviewer ask you whether you would like a drink, whether you would like milk, and how many sugars you take, simply answer the question fully in one go, for example:

'White coffee, two sugars, please'

'Just a glass of water – from a tap would be fine for me, thank you.'

NAVIGATING THE MINEFIELD OF ILLEGAL QUESTIONS

Legal guidelines in the last few years have specifically prohibited certain questions that have no relevance to a candidate's ability to do the job. In theory, interviewers should not ask you about your age, ethnicity, marital status, children or childcare arrangements, birth place, your parents' or partner's occupation, your sexuality, membership of a trade union, hobbies and interests outside of work, or religious beliefs.

However, interviewers rarely ask illegal questions deliberately. They are more likely to be acting out of ignorance. But your choice of answer depends on how much you want the job. You may legally be entitled to refuse to answer the question, but you could possibly embarrass the interviewer and reduce your chances of getting the job. And would you really want to try to prove discrimination in a court of law?

> *Consider how much you want the job. How you deal with illegal interview questions is ultimately up to you. But if you really want the job, you may want to swallow your pride and answer the question anyway.*

'Are you married?'

Of course you want to say: 'None of your bloody business!' But remember that the interviewer probably doesn't realise that he or she is asking an illegal question.

> *'Yes, I'm married. But my other half and I have completely independent careers so please don't think that my marital status would in any way affect my ability to do the job.'*

> *'No, I'm not married. But when or if I ever get married, I can guarantee that it won't affect my work as my career is incredibly important to me.'*

'What happens when you decide to have children?'

Interviewers sometimes assume (incorrectly) that all women want to have children and that children would automatically have an adverse effect on your motivation or ability to work.

'Actually, I have no plans of having children – I don't see myself needing children to be fulfilled.'

'I don't plan on having children for at least five more years, because I have certain career goals that I would like to achieve before I hit 35.'

'I have no current plans to have children. In any case, I wouldn't want a family to slow my career down. I've decided that I want to be a partner within a firm within five years.'

'Are you pregnant at the moment?'

While you do not legally have to disclose the answer to this question, you may want to answer truthfully anyway. An employer could make your life very difficult for you if you lied when you knew that you were expecting.

'I hope you don't mind, but I'd rather not answer that question. Please don't take this the wrong way, but I'm afraid I don't quite see the relevance to my ability to do the job.'

'Yes, I am pregnant. But I hope you will be able to treat me as just another candidate and allow me to demonstrate precisely why I have the right skills for this job.'

'Does your husband/wife/family mind you being away from home?'

The fact that you are married should not affect your willingness to travel. However, avoid getting into a lengthy debate about it and just answer the question in a positive fashion.

'I have always travelled extensively as part of my work – in fact I enjoy it – so my marital status really shouldn't be a cause for concern for you.'

'I'm not married, so this isn't a problem.'

'What hobbies and interests do you have outside of work?'

In theory, an interviewer should not ask you about what you do outside of your work. The legal guidelines say that it shouldn't matter whether you spend all of your leisure time slouched in front of the television or working with charities – the only thing that should matter is your ability to do the job.

However, if you do want to answer the question, try to pick activities that imply you are the kind of person this organisation would want to hire. For example, if the role requires lots of team working, then talking about solitary pursuits such as playing the guitar or going on country walks by yourself could give the wrong impression.

> *Avoid talking about your family excessively as this may give the interviewer the impression that you may not be willing to work long hours when necessary. Mentioning activities to do with your faith or religion has unfortunately also been known to turn some interviewers off.*

'Quite a few of my colleagues at work are also my friends outside of work. So we like to have the occasional drink/meal out/game of football together.'

'I'm a keen photographer. I find that looking for

interesting photos to take gives me a fresh outlook on life
– something that probably helps me to stay more open-
minded about opportunities at work too.'

'Do you play any competitive sports?'

Some interviewers believe that candidates who play team sports
are also more likely to be good team players in the workplace.
But even if you do not play a team sport, it is still better to talk
about some form of exercise that you engage in rather than
nothing at all. Some interviewers worry that people who enjoy
sitting around doing nothing in their leisure time might also sit
around doing nothing in their work time too.

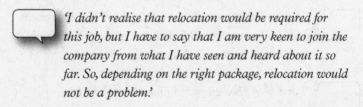

'I play five-a-side football at the weekends. I find that
it helps me to think about the strengths and weaknesses
of different people – it helps me to be a better team
player.'

'I don't play any competitive sports, but I do go jogging
at least twice a week. I find that regular exercise gives me
more energy in my life and my work.'

'Do you have any problems with relocating?'

If relocation is necessary for the job, you should hopefully
already have picked this up in your research. However, if the
question comes as a complete shock to you in the interview, try
to respond in a way that allows you to play for time.

'I didn't realise that relocation would be required for
this job, but I have to say that I am very keen to join the
company from what I have seen and heard about it so
far. So, depending on the right package, relocation would
not be a problem.'

'You only came to this country a few years ago. How are you adjusting to it here?'

Some interviewers may have concerns about the calibre of your language skills. Other interviewers may worry that the fact you're from a different culture may make it more difficult for you to adjust. Either way, you need to reassure interviewers that these are not justified concerns.

'I spent most of my time before I came here working with English-speaking customers anyway, and I'm sure you can tell that my English language skills won't be a barrier to doing a great job here. In terms of settling in, I've found that British employees tend to be less outspoken than the people back home, so I have to ask a few more questions and work harder at listening to get people comfortable with expressing their opinions.'

'This job requires you to work on a Saturday/Sunday – does that cause any conflict with your religion?'

Hopefully you will already have ascertained from your research before the interview that you might have to work on certain days. So if you decided to press ahead with the interview, you should be able to simply say:

'Not at all.'

'Does your religion mean you will need to take more holidays than other employees?'

If you must take certain religious holidays, explain that you will take these as part of your annual leave entitlement.

> 'No. There will be times of the year that I might ideally like to take off. But I'll follow the company's guidelines on the matter and apply for time off just like any other employee.'

'Do you mind if I ask what your partner does for a living?'

Perhaps the interviewer wants to know whether your partner has a demanding job that might cause problems with child care. Or perhaps the interviewer is alluding to your sexuality. In either case, this is an illegal question – although you may still wish to answer the question, albeit in a tangential fashion.

> 'My partner has a demanding career in the airline industry. But I am my own person so what I hope to impress upon you is my ability to do the job on my own merits.'

> Remember that illegal questions are more often asked out of ignorance on the interviewer's part than a deliberate desire to cause offence. In deciding how you will respond to the question, ask yourself: How badly do you want the job?

'Do you have any personal issues that would affect your ability to do the job?'

While this may feel like an intrusive and overly personal question, this is actual a *legal* question for interviewers to ask.

For example, if you had any health problems that would prevent you from doing the job, you should declare them. Similarly, if you have a disability that could impair your ability to do the job, you should say so.

'I hope that I've impressed you with the fact that I possess the interpersonal and financial skills that would allow me to excel in the job. I do have a minor visual impairment which means that I need a special filter on computer screens to help me see them properly. However, government funding would actually cover the cost of that and none of my previous employers have found it to be a major issue at all.'

'I have dyslexia. However, I've found that by typing everything that I do and using a spell check, I can produce written documents that are as good – if not better – than anything that most of my other colleagues can produce. And, if anything, the fact that I've had to deal with this challenge all of my life has made me more hard-working and determined to succeed than many other people. You won't find a more dedicated worker than me.'

'No, I don't have any personal issues that would affect my ability to do the job. Of course I have a family and a personal life, but I've never let anything interfere with my ability to work extremely hard.'

IN SUMMARY...

- Remember that there are many untrained, unskilled interviewers who can ask questions that bear little relation to the job. However, put up with their sometimes strange questions by smiling and trying to turn them to your advantage.

- Aim to give short examples that showcase one of your skills or a personal quality in every answer you give.

- Control your emotions or any anger you may feel when you are asked an illegal question. In the vast majority of cases, the interviewer is asking the question out of ignorance so you must tread carefully so as not to make them feel uncomfortable.

Chapter 8

ANSWERING QUESTIONS ABOUT DIFFERENT STAGES OF YOUR CAREER AND LIFE

In this chapter …
- **Handling questions about school and university**
- **Dealing with questions about returning to work**
- **Talking about age and experience**
- **Handling interview questions aimed specifically at managers**

We all have different experiences as we progress on the journey of life. Some of these experiences are within our control – for example, most of us decide whether to go to university or go into the workforce straight from school. But other experiences may not be within our control – such as being made redundant or having to take time off from work due to illness.

Whatever your age, experience, and personal circumstances, be prepared to explain how your life's journey makes you a strong candidate for the job you are being interviewed for.

HANDLING QUESTIONS ABOUT SCHOOL AND UNIVERSITY

Unsurprisingly, interviewers want to hire people with a good education behind them. So be ready to talk about the decisions you made with respect to your education and your track record of academic achievement as well as how it all makes you a great candidate for the workforce.

If you're reading this book while still at school or university, try to enhance your employability by pursuing opportunities to contribute to projects other than your studies. Try to get involved in committees, clubs, or sports to help you stand out from your peers who have nothing else to talk about other than their academic achievements.

'Why didn't you stay on at school after having completed your GCSEs?'

Make an effort to persuade the employers that you made an active decision to pursue an alternative route. Don't let them think that you 'dropped out' because you aren't bright enough to study.

'I had spent a lot of time around my uncle's car business and had known for some time that I wanted to get into the workplace as soon as possible. I used to get really excited talking to the sales people there and knew that I wanted to do something practical that involved talking to people on a daily basis rather than studying theories in books. However, now that I'm a little older, I'm open-minded about returning to education part-time in order to develop further.'

'What subjects did you most enjoy at school/university?'

Try to draw parallels between your favourite subjects and the job that you're being offered.

'My favourite subject was economics, because I see it as a discipline that permeates just about every aspect of human life, the risks we're willing to take, and business

*and how markets operate. And that's why I want to
develop this understanding further by getting a job
in insurance.'*

'What subjects did you struggle with at school/university?'
Avoid dwelling on what you didn't excel at. This question is the
educational equivalent of 'What is your greatest weakness?' (see
Chapter 5). Make sure to mention only subjects that are not
relevant to the job that you're applying for. For example, saying
that you didn't enjoy learning foreign languages would be fine
so long as the interview isn't for a job that involves a second
language at all.

*'I found it difficult to get motivated studying the science
subjects. I couldn't see how learning about the refraction
of light through a prism or the genetics of fruit flies
would help me in my day-to-day life. I'm much more
interested in the people-oriented subjects such as history,
geography and psychology, and that's what drew me to
this particular vacancy.'*

'Why did you choose the university you went to?'
The interviewer is trying to understand how you make
decisions. Ideally, you would say that you chose your university
in a systematic fashion – after considering a range of course
options and the reputation of different universities, and visiting
campuses to get a feel for the quality of accommodation as well
as social life.

*'I knew that I wanted to study molecular biology so I
researched the top universities offering the degree course.
I got the brochures for the top ten universities and
after reading them decided that only five of them had*

the gap year option available that would offer a year
working in industry. I visited those five universities and
talked to students and some of the staff to get a better
understanding of the courses. And that's how I chose the
ones to apply for. Of course I was very pleased when I got
an offer from my top choice.'

'Why did you choose the degree subject that you studied?'
Again, like the previous question on your choice of university,
the interviewer is interested in your ability to gather data and
make informed decisions. A good response might mention
that you did some research as to the practical nature of the
course and by talking to lecturers and current students as to
the content and relevance of the course to the world outside of
academia. If you can, try to link your degree subject to the job
you're applying for.

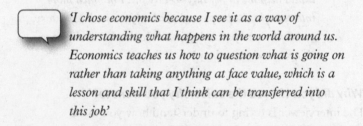

'I chose economics because I see it as a way of
understanding what happens in the world around us.
Economics teaches us how to question what is going on
rather than taking anything at face value, which is a
lesson and skill that I think can be transferred into
this job.'

'I enjoyed chemistry and biology at school so I thought
biochemistry would be a great way to combine both
subjects. When I looked into the subject, I found
that a lot of the work is basically aimed at helping
people to live longer and more satisfying lives. Most
importantly, biochemistry is about having a curiosity
about understanding how things work, which I thought
would be a transferable skill into any occupation.'

'What did you do outside of your studies?'

Employers want to hear that you didn't just do the minimal amount of work so you could spend the rest of your time partying or watching daytime television! Given that many students now have to combine studying with paying their way through their education, you could talk about your paid employment.

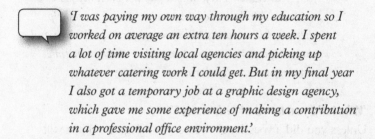

'I was paying my own way through my education so I worked on average an extra ten hours a week. I spent a lot of time visiting local agencies and picking up whatever catering work I could get. But in my final year I also got a temporary job at a graphic design agency, which gave me some experience of making a contribution in a professional office environment.'

Another tactic is to talk about activities you did that helped you to pick up further skills. For example, you may have engaged in team sports that allowed you to develop your teamworking skills. Or you may have worked on a committee that gave you exposure to managing a budget, fund-raising, working with customers, and so on.

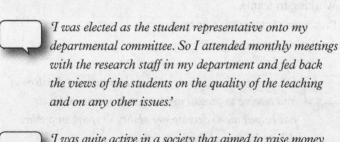

'I was elected as the student representative onto my departmental committee. So I attended monthly meetings with the research staff in my department and fed back the views of the students on the quality of the teaching and on any other issues.'

'I was quite active in a society that aimed to raise money for deprived children in the vicinity of the university. For example, I helped to organise a sponsored fancy dress bike ride through the centre of the city. My role on the committee

on that occasion was actually to deal with the local council and to arrange for the police to cordon off parts of the streets on a Sunday afternoon for our bike route.'

'I was the treasurer of our department's undergraduate society. My job was to organise a recruiting event in the first week of university to ensure that we got lots of first-year students to join and pay up. Then my job was to work with the rest of the committee and try to help them to deliver events like inviting guest speakers in and throwing a party every semester, but at the same time making sure we didn't run out of money.'

'What did you learn at university?'

Unless you did a vocational course, your degree subject will probably be of little interest to the interviewer. Instead, think about the skills that are required for the job. Then give three or four examples of relevant skills that you have picked up from university such as:

- Organising events and your fellow students.
- Raising funds for a society or charity, and managing a budget.
- Working in teams.
- Presenting information at seminars or lectures.
- Analysing data and writing reports.

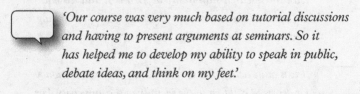

'Our course was very much based on tutorial discussions and having to present arguments at seminars. So it has helped me to develop my ability to speak in public, debate ideas, and think on my feet.'

'I had to write a lot of essays and also did a third-year dissertation. So I've become very good at researching a

topic, analysing the pros and cons of different schools of thought, and presenting information in a sequence that is both logical and interesting.'

'Apart from your degree subject, what transferable skills did you pick up?'

This is similar to the previous question. Again, focus on skills that may be relevant and interesting to the employer.

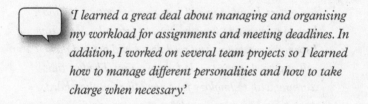

'I learned a great deal about managing and organising my workload for assignments and meeting deadlines. In addition, I worked on several team projects so I learned how to manage different personalities and how to take charge when necessary.'

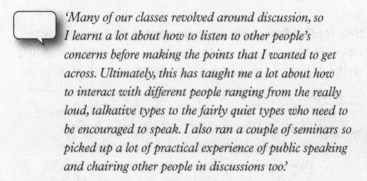

'Many of our classes revolved around discussion, so I learnt a lot about how to listen to other people's concerns before making the points that I wanted to get across. Ultimately, this has taught me a lot about how to interact with different people ranging from the really loud, talkative types to the fairly quiet types who need to be encouraged to speak. I also ran a couple of seminars so picked up a lot of practical experience of public speaking and chairing other people in discussions too.'

'Which parts of your course did you enjoy most?'

Remember that you should answer this question (as with all questions) in a way that demonstrates why you want to work for the employer.

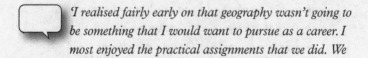

'I realised fairly early on that geography wasn't going to be something that I would want to pursue as a career. I most enjoyed the practical assignments that we did. We

were asked to work in teams of four people, researching
a topic, interviewing people in a town for a survey,
and presenting the results. That's when I decided that
I wanted to work in a team-based environment that
involved a lot of research and working directly with
customers.'

'While I enjoyed learning about economics, I found
that what got me most excited was the work I did with
computers. I taught myself how to write basic code and
how to programme some macros. In fact, a lot of the time
I spent on computers was well above and beyond the
call of what I needed to do for my course. The fact that
working with technology feels more like fun than hard
work brings me to my application to your field.'

'You studied French but you now want to work in law – why?'
Of course this question could have endless variations depending
on the degree you studied and the type of work you want to do.

'I studied French because I was interested in the subject
at school. However, after I did some work experience
working for a small law firm, I discovered that the
day-to-day practice of law was absolutely fascinating.
Law combines so many different skills – from handling
clients and finding out their needs to researching legal
arguments and precedents. And I've now decided that
this would be my dream career.'

'I studied psychology because I have an interest in what
motivates people. And I can think of no better way to
apply that interest in what makes people tick than to
work in a sales and marketing environment

to understand the needs of customers and think of the
best way to get them excited about what your company
can offer them.'

'Why aren't you following the career path suggested by your course?'

Perhaps you studied architecture but don't want to become
an architect. Maybe you studied microbiology but don't want
to work as a scientist. If possible, try to talk about the positive
reasons you want to enter a new career rather than the negative
reasons that put you off from leaving your course of study.

'I enjoyed my degree subject, but by chance I read an article
about management consultancy in the weekend paper. I
was intrigued so I started to do some research into it. And
once I understood the variety of projects that you get in
consultancy as well as the rapid progression that people
can make, I thought that consultancy sounded a lot more
exciting than becoming a physiotherapist.'

'What sort of summer jobs have you had?'

If your previous jobs have no relevance to the role that you are
applying for, you could explain that you took those jobs because
they were the best paying jobs that you could find that fitted
your course schedule. Finish off by sneaking in a skill or quality
that your job taught you.

'I worked as a data entry clerk at Deliveries Express,
a packaging firm. What I learnt was the importance of
team working in a professional environment. When one
member of the team was stretched with too much to do
and I had already finished my tasks, I'd always try to
help out.'

'I worked as a sales assistant at Curby's, a firm of electrical retailers. It was a very customer focused role – I had to listen to their needs and explain the features and benefits of products to persuade them to make a purchase.'

'I think that this role requires a graduate'

Even though you may have the skills and experience for the job, opinions such as this can be quite entrenched. The person screening CVs may have decided that you could do the job – but the person who made that decision may not be the interviewer. Be tactful in trying to change the interviewer's mind. You could try (politely) asking the interviewer: 'I hope you don't mind my asking, but exactly what skills or attributes are you looking for in a graduate applicant?'

When the interviewer responds, you can then compose an answer that shows you have each of those skills or attributes.

'I can understand that university does develop people's ability to learn new concepts and evaluate them critically. However, I have practical experience, which has allowed me to hone these skills. For example, I recently handled a project in which I had to bring in five different potential suppliers. I asked them to pitch what they thought they could do for us and then I had to evaluate the pros and cons of each approach and present to the head of department a critical evaluation of which I thought was the best.'

'Why did you not go to university?'

An employer may want to know what motivated you in the early part of your career. You must endeavour to show the interviewer that, even though you did not go to university, it was not because you do not see the value of learning. In answering this question, you could potentially talk about:

- How personal circumstances meant that you needed to earn a living rather than run up debts studying.
- The fact that you wanted to join the workforce and feel that you were developing practical skills rather than the more abstract and esoteric skills that you might have picked up at university.
- How, at the tender age of 16 or 18, you did not have any interest in or understand the importance of further education. However, in later years, you realised its importance. Then go on to talk about personal improvement that you have undertaken since then – such as diplomas or other courses.

'I really wanted to earn a living. I weighed up the pros and cons of going to university at the time. And given the amount of debt I would have ended up with after a three-year course, I decided not to. I may go back to university later on as a mature student, but only when I am more settled in my career and can do it part-time alongside of my work. What I think I have instead is good work experience and a track record of working well within a team, juggling different priorities and multiple projects at the same time, and coming up with creative solutions to problems.'

'Why did you not finish your course?'

Avoid dwelling on the negative reasons you did not finish your course of study and try instead to focus on what you gained from your decision.

'I went to study a BTEC because everyone else at school was doing it. If I'm honest, I hadn't really thought through the ramifications of further education. It was only when I got there that I realised that I didn't want to do any more studying. I'm very practical and hands-on so I learn by doing tasks rather than studying about them. So I decided not to return to college after the second term and instead to find a job. I'm glad I did because I feel so much more energised knowing that I've got a tangible job to do rather than some theoretical topic to learn about.'

'Why do you have such poor grades?'

If you can't explain your grades away because of difficult circumstances such as a personal illness or family tragedy, try to convince the interviewers that you are simply better suited to doing practical work than study.

'I enjoyed my course of study but unfortunately I've always struggled to cram information into my head so I've never done well in examinations. My reference from my tutor shows that I was much better at the practical side of the course – giving talks to the other people in my tutorial group and debating issues. And given that this job is of a very practical nature rather than requiring me to commit lots of facts to memory, I know that I can excel in it.'

You may be tempted to lie about your grades in future job applications. But be extremely careful as such facts are very easily checked by employers!

'What further education do you think you may need?'

If you are further along in your career, you may want to think about continuing your professional development. Make sure you investigate in your research before you attend any interview whether people who end up in this kind of job tend to pursue any particular qualifications.

'I've been working in healthcare for six years now so I think the time may be right to think about refreshing my skill set by doing an NVQ in healthcare management. I've been looking into it and it's something that I could do in the evenings and weekends without it affecting my work – and it would make me a much better contributor to the team.'

'In order to fulfil my ambition of moving into a more generalist role, I realise that I need to sharpen up my financial understanding of the business so I'm thinking of taking a part-time master's course in financial management.'

'How would you feel about pursuing further qualifications in the future?'

Whether you're 16 or 60, you may still have to prove that you're willing to learn and grow at work. Your research about the nature of the job should uncover whether you might be expected to study for further qualifications in the future. So make sure you are prepared to tell the interviewers what they feel they want to hear.

'I'm genuinely quite excited about the prospect of studying for the diploma in social policy. I read on your website that you offer an annual sum to go towards

approved courses. This would be a great investment in
my career, given that I plan to be in this field for the very
long-term.'

'Given that you have only very limited work experience, what do you think the key challenges will be in working for us?'

Employers often tell me that some of the graduates and school leavers they take on don't really know what it takes to succeed in the modern workplace. So reassure them that you're willing to do whatever work you're given, but that you're also keen to learn and progress.

'I realise that I only have a couple of weeks of work
experience from having waited on tables in a restaurant
rather than having worked in an office environment.
However, I can assure you that I follow instruction very
well so would have no problems doing whatever tasks I'm
given. Also, I was used to working very long shifts at the
restaurant, often until one or two o'clock in the morning,
so I hope that further demonstrates my willingness to put
in whatever hours it takes to do well in my career.'

'Can you tell me how you keep up with industry trends?'

Employers are always keen to know that candidates are making an effort to learn, develop, and educate themselves. There are other ways to continue your professional development that aren't necessarily linked to courses and qualifications.

'I subscribe to Pharmacy Today *to make sure that I*
know all the latest about legal changes in the prescription
of drugs. I also attend the annual conference down in
Brighton and go along specifically to hear what new
developments are going on. I'm also still in touch with

a lot of my friends from college who now run pharmacies all over the country and we all exchange ideas about how we can do our jobs better.'

HANDLING YOUR RETURN TO WORK

Interviewers sometimes worry that people who have been out of work may lack the motivation to work hard again. Whether you were made redundant, took maternity leave, took time off to bring up a family or to recuperate from an illness, be ready to prove to employers that you are serious and committed about re-joining the workforce and helping the organisation to achieve its goals.

'Were you made redundant?'

Redundancy used to have much more of a stigma attached to it 20 or even ten years ago. But today's job climate is very different – there is no such thing as a 'job for life' anymore. Honesty may therefore be the best policy.

'Yes. The company needed to reduce its headcount by 15 percent. There were nearly 200 job losses in the UK alone, and that's why I find myself looking for a new job.'

'Why did they select you for redundancy?'

This question may be a sneaky attempt to check that you really were made redundant as opposed to being fired for poor performance or disciplinary problems. When making staff redundant, many companies have a simple policy of 'last in, first out'. So, if you can, say that you were simply selected because you (and the others who were also made redundant) had a shorter tenure than the remaining members of the team.

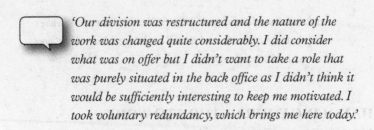

'Our division was restructured and the nature of the work was changed quite considerably. I did consider what was on offer but I didn't want to take a role that was purely situated in the back office as I didn't think it would be sufficiently interesting to keep me motivated. I took voluntary redundancy, which brings me here today.'

'Why have you been out of work for so long?'

Finding a job takes time. But being out of work is often a good opportunity for many candidates to evaluate their goals in life and think about what they really want to be doing for the rest of their careers.

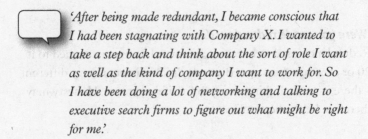

'After being made redundant, I became conscious that I had been stagnating with Company X. I wanted to take a step back and think about the sort of role I want as well as the kind of company I want to work for. So I have been doing a lot of networking and talking to executive search firms to figure out what might be right for me.'

'You've been away from work for some time – how have you spent your time?'

Try to show that you have not simply been sitting at home watching daytime television all the time! Possibly the best answer is to talk about any independent study you did or course you attended to keep your mind active.

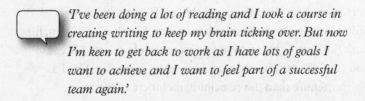

'I've been doing a lot of reading and I took a course in creating writing to keep my brain ticking over. But now I'm keen to get back to work as I have lots of goals I want to achieve and I want to feel part of a successful team again.'

Feel free to talk about any projects or work you completed too – such as having worked part-time or as an unpaid volunteer for any charitable or other causes.

'I'm worried that your time away from the workforce may put you at a disadvantage'

The interviewer may be worried that the reasons that took you out of work (e.g. young children, illness, or failure to find a job) may crop up again in the future. Begin by asking: 'If you don't mind me asking, what is it exactly that worries you?'

Once you understand the interviewer's concerns, you can counter them.

'I can assure you that I'm fully recovered from the virus that had hit me so hard. I got a clean bill of health last month and I'm willing to put in long hard days again. I know that this kind of job will require quite a lot of flexibility in working hours and I want to assure you that I can handle the workload.'

'I can see your thinking, but I believe that my time away from work has actually made me a stronger candidate. We both know that the job is quite demanding. And given that I've had six months off to enjoy my family life, I can say with my hand on my heart that I'm genuinely looking forward to the challenge of throwing all of my energies into my work again.'

'You've been working for yourself for some time now – why do you want to be employed by someone again?'

Not strictly a question that fits into the category of 'returning to work' and perhaps more a case of changing the type of work you do. But still a question that interviewers ask of people who have spent any time working freelance or as independent consultants. Many interviewers assume that setting up in business on one's own is a way to make more money – so anyone who decides to re-join a company must have failed to succeed at it.

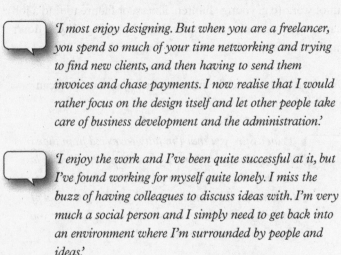

'I most enjoy designing. But when you are a freelancer, you spend so much of your time networking and trying to find new clients, and then having to send them invoices and chase payments. I now realise that I would rather focus on the design itself and let other people take care of business development and the administration.'

'I enjoy the work and I've been quite successful at it, but I've found working for myself quite lonely. I miss the buzz of having colleagues to discuss ideas with. I'm very much a social person and I simply need to get back into an environment where I'm surrounded by people and ideas.'

DEALING WITH QUESTIONS ABOUT AGE AND EXPERIENCE

Changes to employment legislation mean that you no longer have to put your age on your CV. So it may be the case that you could find yourself at an interview up against candidates who are considerably younger or older than you.

If that happens, be prepared to stand your ground and explain why you would make a great candidate in spite of (or perhaps because of) your age. An interviewer may be concerned that an older candidate does not have the drive and motivation of a younger candidate. Conversely, an interviewer may feel that younger candidates may lack the sophistication and maturity of older ones.

In stating your case, remember to express your disagreement tactfully with the interviewer. Making a stand against age discrimination may make you feel better from a moral standpoint and further the cause of equal rights, but it probably won't help your chances of getting the job.

'How old are you?'

You don't legally have to answer this question. However, doing so could make you appear somewhat confrontational. How you deal with the question is ultimately dependent on how much you want the job.

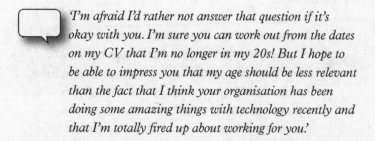

'I'm afraid I'd rather not answer that question if it's okay with you. I'm sure you can work out from the dates on my CV that I'm no longer in my 20s! But I hope to be able to impress you that my age should be less relevant than the fact that I think your organisation has been doing some amazing things with technology recently and that I'm totally fired up about working for you.'

'I'll be 24 on my next birthday. Perhaps you're thinking that I'm a bit younger than the ideal candidate you may have had in mind. But I've been working since I was 12 years old when I first got a paper round. I've worked in many school and university holidays as well and in my last job was already managing a team of two people – both

of whom were older than me. I'm therefore confident that I have the maturity to deal with the demands of this role.'

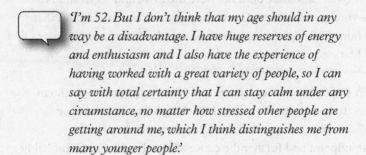

'I'm 52. But I don't think that my age should in any way be a disadvantage. I have huge reserves of energy and enthusiasm and I also have the experience of having worked with a great variety of people, so I can say with total certainty that I can stay calm under any circumstance, no matter how stressed other people are getting around me, which I think distinguishes me from many younger people.'

'This is a challenging role – are you sure you want to do it at this stage of your career?'

If you can, respond by saying that you feel you still have personal goals that you have yet to achieve and that there is still this one (or perhaps more) challenge(s) that you need to complete so that you can feel that you have achieved your career ambitions.

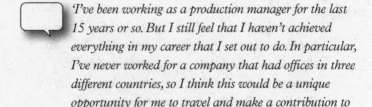

'I've been working as a production manager for the last 15 years or so. But I still feel that I haven't achieved everything in my career that I set out to do. In particular, I've never worked for a company that had offices in three different countries, so I think this would be a unique opportunity for me to travel and make a contribution to the business at the same time.'

'When do you plan to retire?'

Interviewers like to feel that they are going to get good value out of the people that they hire. They don't want to hear that you are only going to stick around for one or two years. So the best answer, if you are able to give it, would be:

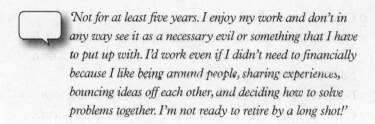

'Not for at least five years. I enjoy my work and don't in any way see it as a necessary evil or something that I have to put up with. I'd work even if I didn't need to financially because I like being around people, sharing experiences, bouncing ideas off each other, and deciding how to solve problems together. I'm not ready to retire by a long shot!'

'Do you think you have the maturity to do this job?'

The best way to demonstrate your maturity is to give an example of how you have dealt with similar challenges to the ones that may be required of you in this role.

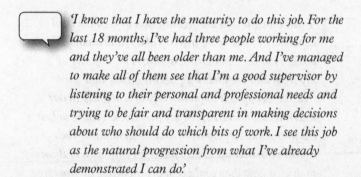

'I know that I have the maturity to do this job. For the last 18 months, I've had three people working for me and they've all been older than me. And I've managed to make all of them see that I'm a good supervisor by listening to their personal and professional needs and trying to be fair and transparent in making decisions about who should do which bits of work. I see this job as the natural progression from what I've already demonstrated I can do.'

DEALING WITH QUESTIONS AIMED AT MANAGERS AND SUPERVISORS

Managers have to interact with their teams in a very different way to how employees work together.

'Are you a good manager?'

Does the interviewer expect you to say 'no'? Rather than just answering 'yes', treat this as if it were a competency-based question. Provide an example to explain why you are a good manager. Perhaps you could talk about a situation such as:

- Coaching or developing the employees in your team.
- Splitting up an initially overwhelming task into different roles and responsibilities for the members of your team, and then helping them to complete the task.
- Being brought in to turn around an underperforming team.
- Creating a vision or business strategy for your department.
- Inspiring or motivating a team to achieve results.

Your reply should incorporate a brief explanation of the background to the example, as well as a description of what you did and the results achieved.

'I was brought into the organisation to turn the legal department from being a group of administrators into advisors to the other business units. The majority of my team had been there for over a decade and were reactive as opposed to proactively offering help to our internal customers. I spent my first weeks getting to know the individuals in my team and understanding their aspirations. I set up weekly meetings with each of them to discuss how they could be more proactive in providing advice to our internal customers. Over about six months, we've had some really good feedback from the other business units.'

'What do you see as the difference between being a manager and a leader?'

The fashion in recent years has been for more and more organisations to seek out leaders (who are supposed to be inspirational) rather than managers (who are sometimes perceived as rather dictatorial in style).

'I've heard it said that managers do things right while leaders do the right thing. To answer your question, leaders are typically thought of as being more inspirational and focused on the big picture while managers are sometimes thought of as authoritarian and operational or even small-minded. I think that elements of both are important for running a good organisation. You need to be inspirational and able to think of the long-term future, but at the same time you have to be aware of what's going on and make sure that nothing slips through the cracks.'

'What skills do you think are needed to be a good people manager?'

There is no one right answer to this question. As an organisational psychologist, I often run leadership development programmes for businesses and I teach that there are five skills to being a good leader:

■ Self-awareness – the ability to seek feedback in order to understand your own strengths and weaknesses.

■ Empowerment – being able to not only give people responsibility and coach them to find their own best ways of solving problems and doing tasks.

■ Relationship building – the skill of developing human relationships with people rather than treating members of the team as mere employees.

■ Vision – the ability to develop and communicate an inspiring picture of the future.

■ Ethics and integrity – being as honest, open and trustworthy as possible.

> *'Clearly lots of skills are important and I can talk you through them in as much detail as you want. But for me, the critical one is being able to coach people by asking people questions rather than giving them solutions all of the time.'*

'How would you describe your style of management?'

Your response should be dictated in large part by your research and understanding of the industry and style of management that may be required in this organisation. For example, while some organisations are very disciplined (e.g. in the oil or airline industry in which mistakes could cost lives) other organisations may be much more willing to take risks.

> *'I'm a strong believer in following rules. I like to explain tasks to members of my team and I check that they understand exactly what it is that they need to do. I set deadlines for the delivery of pieces of work and monitor closely their progress so that I can deal with problems before they occur.'*

> *'I try to be very open-minded and I invite members of my team to come up with their own ideas for how to get work done. I try to avoid being prescriptive as I believe my job is to help people to grow and become more capable so that eventually they can take over my job.'*

'Tell me how you coached or developed someone in your team'

Many organisations feel that coaching is a key skill that supervisors and managers must be able to demonstrate.

> *'I had someone in my team who was technically very good at his job but didn't always speak up in meetings.*

I knew he could make a much bigger contribution to the team so started to encourage him to take on additional bits of work that I knew would boost his confidence. I also sent him on an internal training course to do with becoming more assertive and he said he got a lot out of that. I also took him along to some internal meetings with my boss so he could get wider exposure to the workings of the broader organisation. Over the last year or so, I'm proud to say that he is now my deputy and the person I trust most in my team.'

'Describe a tough time that you had in dealing with a member of your team'

Don't fall into the trap of saying that you never had any problems in your entire career – no interviewer will believe you. The interviewer is looking for you to talk openly about how you tackled a difficult situation with an employee. But be careful, as the worst thing that you could say here is that you used your seniority to force the member of your team to do it your way. Try to finish your example on a high note if you can though.

'There was someone else in the team who didn't seem to be very motivated in her work. I tried to coach her and to find projects that would excite her. But she just didn't respond. I liked her as a person but it was unfair on the rest of the team, so in the end I had to get personnel involved and we took her through a disciplinary process. We gave her three months and various formal warnings to work a bit harder, but she didn't respond. Ultimately, we had to move her on. We've not managed to replace her yet, but I've noticed that the morale within the team is already much better as they don't feel that anyone is letting the team down now.'

'Which leader has inspired you and why?'

Your safest bet is to pick a famous leader from at least several decades ago that most people agree was a great and inspirational leader such as Martin Luthor King Junior, John F. Kennedy, Winston Churchill, and so on – rather than a more contemporary figure who may be more contentious.

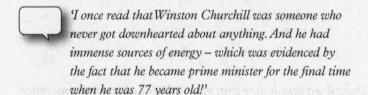

'I once read that Winston Churchill was someone who never got downhearted about anything. And he had immense sources of energy – which was evidenced by the fact that he became prime minister for the final time when he was 77 years old!'

An alternative tactic would be to talk about a manager you've come across that impressed you.

'In my previous job, I worked for a managing director who commanded such respect. Even when people around him let him down badly, he never lost his temper and had an incredible ability to listen to other people's concerns. I've tried to learn from his example by staying calm and making a supreme effort to listen to others before I put across my point of view.'

IN SUMMARY...

- Understand that interviewers sometimes worry about candidates who do not have a standard career history.
- Be prepared to answer questions about why you are different from the 'average' candidate. Think about the doubts that the interviewer has about you at your stage of your career and rehearse some answers for the sort of questions that the interviewer could ask you.
- If you have experience of managing other people, be ready to talk about specific managerial skills such as how you have developed others and coped with performance issues.

Chapter 9

ASKING THE RIGHT QUESTIONS

In this chapter ...
- **Preparing intelligent questions**
- **Exploring the nature of the work**
- **Asking about the future**
- **Finding out about the culture of the organisation**
- **Avoiding questions that create the wrong impression**

At some point during the proceedings, the interviewer may ask: 'Do you have any questions?'

Interviewers frequently judge candidates on the nature of the questions that are asked. Do you ask about the pay and benefits? Are you focused on the day-to-day demands of the role? Or are you more interested in opportunities for promotion and enhanced responsibility? Different questions give interviewers different impressions about your motivations.

This chapter contains many examples of questions for you to tailor to the different interviewers and employers that you will meet. Not all of them will be appropriate for every situation, so think ahead and choose carefully.

> *Remember that this is your opportunity to find more out about the job and the company. If the interviewer were to offer you the job, would you have enough information to decide whether to accept or not?*

DOING YOUR RESEARCH TO FIND OUT THE RIGHT QUESTIONS TO ASK EVERY TIME

Intelligent and thoughtful questions can demonstrate to an interviewer that you had the motivation and interest to do your research on the organisation. However, when preparing a list of questions to ask your prospective employer, make sure that your questions could not have been answered in any other way. Many companies provide information in recruitment brochures, websites, job descriptions and other materials as well as the original job advert. If you ask a question that could have been answered in any of these other sources of information, you will come across as poorly prepared.

For example, it may be a valid question to ask Company A about their plans for growth – however, Company B may have published a lengthy statement about their expansion plans on their website. Accordingly, be careful that your questions are relevant for the particular company that you are being interviewed by. If you simply take the same list of questions to different interviewers, you risk ruining your chances.

Understanding broad guidelines around your questions

Your research may uncover dozens and dozens of questions that you might want to ask. However, asking too many questions could annoy your interviewer – especially if he or she has arranged to interview a number of candidates and is running behind schedule. Here are some rules of thumb for asking questions:

■ Ask at least two or three questions in every interview to show that you have done your research and are interested in finding out more about the company.

- Think about the time slot that has been allocated for your interview. If you know that you are supposed to finish at 4.30pm and it's already 4.25pm, you know that your questions should be fairly few in number.
- For most roles, avoid asking more than half-a-dozen questions during the interview itself. Should you be offered the job, you could always arrange to come back to meet the interviewer or other people within the organisation to have your questions answered.

> *Bear in mind that the number of questions you can ask should be broadly related to the seniority of the job. If you are applying for an entry-level role, an interviewer will probably expect you to ask only a handful of questions. For a managing director's role, you may need to schedule another appointment to come back to have all of your questions answered.*

SHOWING AN INTEREST IN THE WORK ITSELF

There are many questions that you could ask about the role. However, remember to check that the questions you do choose to ask could not have been answered in your research.

Questions to ask could include:

- 'What are the day-to-day duties involved in this job?'
- 'How will my performance be measured?'
- 'How are targets set? How much say would I have in setting them?'
- 'How much contact would I have in this role with clients/customers/suppliers/finance/marketing/sales/etcetera?'
- 'Who will I report to?'
- 'Who would I be spending most of my working time with?'

- 'Who are the key decision makers that I would need to get along with? And how would you describe each of them?'
- 'What do you see as the immediate challenges for me if I were to be given the job?'
- 'What do you most enjoy about working here?'

You might also want to find out more about why the employer is looking to fill this role:

- 'Why has this vacancy arisen?'
- 'What happened to the previous job holder?'
- 'Are you looking for anything in particular from the person who will take this role?'
- 'How do you see this role developing?'
- 'How quickly are you looking for someone to take on this role?'

Asking questions about managerial roles

If you are going to be supervising or managing others, you may want to consider questions such as:

- 'What's the make-up of the current team?'
- 'What do you see as the challenges in helping the team to be more successful?'
- 'Are there any star performers or difficult people within the team that need special attention?'
- 'How much scope would I have to change the people within the team?'
- 'What sort of budget would I have for running the team?'

Asking questions about the broader team and organisation

You could also ask questions about the structure and current challenges facing the company as a whole:

- 'How is the department that I would be joining viewed by the rest of the organisation?'
- 'How is the company structured?'
- 'When was the last company restructuring? And how did it affect this department?'
- 'What challenges is the organisation currently facing?'
- 'What are the new initiatives/projects/campaigns that the team is working on?'

Or if you have an insight into how the company is perceived against its competitors, these could also be good questions to ask as it can show off the research that you have done. For example: 'I read in the papers that your competitor, Company X, has just launched a new service line. What's the view in your company on it? And how are you going to react to it?'

Be careful: there's a fine line between demonstrating an interest in the job and asking questions to show off.

EXPLORING THE FUTURE AND DEMONSTRATING YOUR COMMITMENT

I have already mentioned the fact that employers usually want to recruit employees who will stay for at least two to three years. So it may be worth your while to ask some questions about the future.

For example, you could ask about your own future with the organisation:

- 'What training and development is given to employees?'
- 'What opportunities are there for promotion?'
- 'How does the company promote personal growth?'

- 'What kind of career paths have other people taken after coming in at this level?'
- 'Do people move between offices much?'
- 'What opportunities are there for working abroad with the company?'

Asking more questions about the broader organisation

You might also want to ask about the company's prospects:

- 'What are the organisation's long-term objectives?'
- 'How has the firm been performing in recent months?'
- 'What are the company's plans for growth? And how will it achieve these?'
- 'What new products/services is the company planning to launch?'
- 'Are any organisational changes planned in the near future?'

ASKING ABOUT THE ORGANISATION'S CULTURE

No matter how informative the website and other official sources of information, you need to be able to talk to people about the culture – the way in which people behave towards each other on a day-to-day basis.

Some general questions to ask:

- 'How would you describe the culture of the organisation?'
- 'What's the best thing about working for this organisation?'
- 'Why did you decide to join the company?'
- 'What most frustrates you about working here?'
- 'How would you describe the management style around here?'
- 'What does it take to succeed around here?'

- 'Could you tell me about the sort of people who have failed here? What was it they did or didn't do that made them unsuccessful?'

Or you could use questions to probe on more specific issues:

- 'Would you describe this as a political organisation? And if so, why?'
- 'Is there much inter-departmental rivalry in the company?'
- 'How would you describe the company's attitude to risk taking?'
- 'How does the company respond to new threats and opportunities?'
- 'How much autonomy and latitude are people given in the organisation?'
- 'How much do people socialise together outside of work?'

Avoid asking too many questions in quick-fire succession. Bear in mind that the tone of your questions should be conversational – this isn't an interrogation!

AVOIDING CERTAIN QUESTIONS UNTIL YOU HAVE AN OFFER ON THE TABLE

There may be certain burning questions that you really want to ask and have answered, but you do not want to jeopardise leaving the interviewer with the wrong sort of impression. So it may be better to avoid certain areas of discussion until you have a firm job offer.

Topics to stay away from therefore include:

- Pay, benefits and annual leave allowances.
- Criteria and process for being awarded pay rises.

- Flexible working practices such as working from home or maternity/paternity leave.
- The workload, the length of the working day, and general requirements to do overtime.

IN SUMMARY...

- Do your research and prepare a list of questions specifically for each employer. Check that none of your questions could have been answered by the organisation's website or other materials.
- Focus most of your questions on the role and responsibilities of the job. Make sure to ask at least one question about how you could develop in the role too.
- Remember that an interview is a two-way process – it's as much an opportunity for you to find out whether you want the job as for the organisation to figure out whether they want you.
- Steer clear of questions on money, the hours, and other topics that could inadvertently make you appear greedy or lazy.

Chapter 10

SUCCEEDING WITH PSYCHOMETRIC TESTS, ASSESSMENT CENTRES, AND OTHER TYPES OF INTERVIEW

In this chapter ...
- **Passing psychometric tests**
- **Dealing with assessment centre exercises**
- **Dealing with panel and group interviews**
- **Handling telephone interviews**
- **Handling video interviews**

Employers are a sneaky bunch. With every year, more and more employers are using techniques such as psychometric tests, assessment centres, and panel interviewers to weed out weak candidates and only hire the very best.

This chapter explains what each of these trials means for you and gives you advice on performing to the best of your ability. There are also some example psychometric test questions in this chapter to help you practise for the real thing!

DEALING WITH PSYCHOMETRIC TESTS

Many candidates fear the prospect of being subjected to psychometric tests. But there is no need to be afraid if you understand their purpose. There are actually two distinct categories of psychometric tests:

1. Personality questionnaires, which measure preferences and motivations. These try to measure how you generally like

to behave in certain situations. What do you like or dislike?
These do not have right or wrong answers, although the
employer may be looking for candidates who have a certain
'type' of personality.

2. Aptitude tests, which measure skills and abilities. Aptitude
   tests do have right or wrong answers.

Presenting your positive side in personality tests

Personality questionnaires can take many different shapes and
forms. Many are presented as pencil-and-paper questions for
you to complete. However, more and more organisations are
using computerised or online tests that ask you simply to type
your responses.

Some questionnaires may ask you to tick or circle whether you
'agree' or 'disagree' with a number of questions. Others may ask
you to respond whether you 'strongly agree', 'agree', 'disagree',
or 'strongly disagree' with a series of statements. Some may ask
you to write your answers directly on the question book, while
others may ask you to circle your answers on a separate answer
sheet. So read the instructions carefully to make sure that you
do not make a fool of yourself.

There's no point practising personality tests as they are rarely
timed. However, follow these two key tips to give yourself the
best chance of impressing the employer:

■ **Be very careful of trying to second-guess personality
questionnaires**. Different personality questionnaires
measure different dimensions of personality and it can be very
difficult to know exactly what the interviewers are looking for.
For example, you might assume that a particular job requires
employees who are very extroverted. But this employer might

have looked at previous employees and discovered in their research that the extremely extroverted employees tend to get bored and leave quickly. So the interviewers may in fact prefer employees who are less extroverted. You cannot tell what the 'right' answer may be. Consequently, you may distort your responses in the wrong direction. Giving responses that you think the interviewer is looking for could ruin your chances of getting the job. It's better to jot down your honest answers.

■ **Give yourself the benefit of the doubt in answering the questions**.

In an interview, you don't automatically have to confess all of your flaws. So neither should you be too critical of yourself when completing a personality questionnaire.

When answering personality test questions, be kind to yourself and see yourself as your mother or best friend might see you.

Scoring highly on aptitude tests

Aptitude tests are frequently used as a predictor of on-the-job performance. They are often also called 'ability tests' or 'cognitive tests'. Most commonly, these are used to measure numeracy or verbal reasoning skills. However, for technical jobs, employers may also try to assess skills such as spatial reasoning or abstract reasoning. Speed and accuracy are essential, so make sure that you:

■ **Read the instructions thoroughly**. Most of the errors made by candidates are made because they did not read the instructions carefully enough. Take note of any unusual directions. For example, one test might ask you to put a pen tick in a box for the answer that you think is right, whereas another test might ask you to completely fill in a circle using pencil.

- **Identify how the scoring works**. For example, some aptitude tests take marks off if you make mistakes, so it may be worth working slowly but accurately. Other tests simply add on marks for each question that you did correctly – so it may be worth guessing the answers to a few questions if you are running out of time.
- **Keep an eye on the time**. Most aptitude tests are timed. It may be worth doing a quick mental calculation before you tackle the individual questions to see how long you should spend on each question. For example, if there are 60 questions in total to be completed in 45 minutes, then if you struggle with any question for more than a minute, you should definitely move on. If you do not usually wear a watch, it may be worth borrowing one or taking a small timer along with you to an interview in case the employer should spring an aptitude test on you.

Look online for free *aptitude tests that you can practise on. Try typing the phrase 'aptitude test questions' into a search engine such as www.google.com and you will get dozens of relevant hits.*

Aptitude tests are designed to be difficult, so try not to worry too much about questions that you do not understand and are forced to skip. Most employers specifically design their aptitude tests so that average candidates will be allowed to make maybe several dozen mistakes and still pass the test. Even the brightest and best candidates will still make a few mistakes.

Enhancing your skill with psychometric tests

You don't need to practise personality tests because they're not timed and they're difficult to fake anyway. But here are two short aptitude tests with ten questions each for you to practise on. Do these *without* a calculator, as you won't be allowed a calculator if an employer asks you to do a test. You'll find the answers to this in the appendix located at the back of the book. Good luck!

Psychometric Test 1

Calculate the answers to each of the following questions:

1. A household's electricity bill comes to £184.50 and is charged at 15 pence a unit. How many units of electricity did the household use?

2. The same household's water bill this year was £200. However, it has been estimated that the bill will increase by 12 percent next year. How much will the household have to pay for its water bill next year?

3. An office worker who gets paid £5.50 an hour filled in a time sheet claiming that she had worked 38 hours in the first week in January. How much did she get paid that week?

4. A plane is due to depart at 15.15 hours. Passengers are required to check in two and a half hours before departure. One particular passenger needs to leave two hours to travel to the airport. What time does this passenger need to leave the house?

5. The printer connected to your computer in the office can print 15 black and white pages in a minute and eight colour pages in a minute. How many minutes will it take to print a 208-page colour document?

6. A father has £109 in his pocket. He lends £14 to his son and gives a further £27 to his daughter. How much money does the father have left in his pocket?

7. A survey conducted by a fizzy drinks maker found that one quarter of people most enjoyed the apple flavour of their drink. The survey also found that one in eight people most enjoyed the orange flavour of their drink. What fraction of people preferred neither the apple nor orange flavours?

8 A computer hard drive spins 418 times a minute. How many times does it spin in an hour?

9. A bank pays an interest rate of 5 percent on its savings accounts. How much compound interest will the bank need to pay out on £2,000 invested for three years?

10. A plumber estimates that a particular job will cost £200 plus VAT at 17.5 percent. How much VAT needs to be paid?

Psychometric Test 2

For each question, choose the letter A, B, C, or D that most closely represents the answer to each question:

1. In 2004, a survey found that 70 percent of school leavers had poor language skills. If there were 800 school leavers in the survey, how many of the school leavers were found to have poor language skills?
   A 600　　　　B 580　　　　C 560　　　　D 540

2. A colleague dispatched 17 parcels at a cost of £18 each and 14 parcels at a cost of £9 each. What was the total cost of

sending all 31 parcels?

A £837   B £126   C £306   D £432

3. Your boss has to catch a flight from the airport at 19.15.
She has to arrive at the airport two hours beforehand and
her train journey to the airport will take her three-and-a-half
hours. What time must she catch her train?

A 14.00   B 14.15   C 13.45   D 13.30

4. A metre of electrical cabling costs 39 pence. How much
would 120 metres cost?

A £46.80   B £48.80   C £50.80   D £59.60

5. A group of four friends all put £10 each into a fund to buy
leaving presents for a colleague. If the colleague received
three presents worth £8.60, £9.15, and £21.20, how much
was left in the fund?

A £1.35   B £1.05   C £1.15   D £1.20

6. If a scientist's gyroscope spins 300 times a minute, how
many times does it spin in an hour?

A 18,000   B 180,000   C 1,800   D 90,000

7. On her son's 15th birthday, a mother puts £400 into a bank
account for her son. The bank pays 15 percent interest a year.
How much could the son withdraw on his 18th birthday?

A £628.35   B £618.65   C £608.45   D £608.35

8. A wealthy individual pays 45 percent tax on his annual income
of £45,000. How much does he get to take home after tax?

A £26,250   B £24,250   C £24,750   D £24,500

9. A pack of eight highlighter pens costs £7.68. What is the

cost of three highlighter pens?

A £1.92   B £2.88   C £0.96   D £1.68

10. A survey found that one in four supermarket shoppers described themselves as 'very satisfied' with the price of its goods. If 128 people were surveyed, how many of the shoppers were not 'very satisfied' with the price of its goods?

A 90   B 96   C 92   D 32

THRIVING AT ASSESSMENT CENTRES

Assessment centres are an increasingly popular way for employers to assess the skills of candidates. Rather than simply asking candidates to talk about their skills, the interviewers may want to put you through your paces by asking you to demonstrate your skills rather than merely talk about them in an interview.

The term 'assessment centre' simply refers to any selection method that may ask you to sort through a mock in-tray, give a presentation, get involved in a group exercise with other candidates, or even engage in a role play scenario.

Handling in-tray exercises

In-tray exercises try to simulate the typical demands that you might face at your desk if you were to be successful in joining the company. You might be presented with a pile of memos, faxes, reports, and other correspondence requiring your attention. Increasingly, organisations are using electronic in-trays, simulating your email inbox too.

For example, the instructions may read: 'It is Monday today, the first day in your new job. It is 9am and you have taken over from the previous manager who left only last Friday. Unfortunately, your predecessor did not clear his desk before leaving the company, and it is up to you to deal with all of the remaining correspondence.'

You may be asked to read the documents and respond in writing to a certain number of tasks. Here are some tips for managing the masses of information that comprise the typical in-tray exercise:

- **Read the instructions extremely carefully**. The instructions may ask you to deal with every single item within the in-tray – for example, to write a reply to every fax, email, and letter you receive. Or the instructions may ask you to pick out only a certain number of the most important items. You can never know what the exercise may require you to do so read the instructions and perhaps use a highlighter pen to help you pick out the most critical points to keep in mind.

- **Skim-read all of the information quickly**. Most in-tray exercises contain both critical information as well as distracting items that are designed to lead weaker candidates astray. Avoid responding to individual items until you have spent a few minutes glancing at everything to give you a sense of what information you are provided with.

- **Sort all of the items into three categories**:
  1. Important *and* urgent items – consider the instructions for handling the in-tray and try to pick out the key 'A' issues that you must deal with during the in-tray exercise. For example, there may be a letter from a large customer that needs immediate attention in order to retain business for your employer.
  2. Important but less urgent items – create a 'B' list of items that you will get round to handling only when you have

handled your 'A' list items. For example, there may be a letter that also needs immediate attention – but one that comes from a smaller customer that your employer might deem slightly less important.

3. Less important items – create a list of 'C' items which should only merit your attention if you have dealt with the first two categories of items. In reality, in-tray exercises are usually designed so that you won't have time to handle all of these. But that's fine so long as you handle all of your 'A' and 'B' priority items first. For example, there may be a minor complaint from a supplier that – even if it isn't handled immediately – probably wouldn't cause your employer to lose money any time soon.

Giving high-impact presentations

Increasingly, employers are looking for candidates with good oral communication and presentation skills. Some employers ask candidates to prepare a presentation beforehand, while others prefer to give candidates a topic to present during the day of the assessment centre itself.

You can improve your performance during the presentation element of any assessment centre by preparing in the following ways:

■ **Structure your presentation**. There is an adage that says 'tell the audience what you are going to say, say it, then remind them what you said.' Begin with a short introduction to the topic before the main body of your presentation. And end with a short summary of the key points of the presentation. It's always better to have a short presentation with a logical flow rather than try to cram too much information into a presentation.

- **Use simple visual aids**. Candidates who choose simply to speak without visual aids can be quite boring to watch. Visual aids provide something else for the audience to focus on.
- **Use bullet points in your visual aids**. Visual aids should be clear and uncluttered. Your visual aids are there to *aid* your presentation – they should not *be* your presentation. If appropriate, draw a simple graph or diagram to help make your presentation more visually arresting.
- **Watch the time**. Your instructions will give you strict instructions on your allotted time – so make sure that you stick to it. Also read the instructions carefully to see if you are expected to leave time to invite questions from the audience as well.

> ***Keep your visual aids simple.*** *If you have a choice, use either flip charts and coloured pens or overhead transparencies. The assessors are trying to evaluate your confidence and communication skill rather than your technical skill with high-tech solutions such as slide projectors or computer PowerPoint that are far more likely to go wrong.*

Thinking fast for group discussions

Interviewers often ask a group of candidates to discuss a topic for a certain length of time. You can't prepare for the precise topic. But you *can* practise the skill of thinking quickly of things to say.

Below are some sample topics. If you like, you could practise preparing for them. Simply pick a topic and give yourself five to ten minutes to prepare some pros and cons to contribute to a possible discussion..

- 'Some parents have suggested that schools should teach more science and technology-related topics such as computer programming. This would mean less teaching of traditional subjects such as history and foreign languages. What are the arguments both for and against introducing more science-based teaching?'
- 'The UK government is considering doing away with the British pound and adopting the Chinese yuan as its national currency. Discuss.'
- 'Doctors in many countries have argued that patients who are obese should be forced to lose weight before being given expensive operations such as organ transplants. What are your views on this issue?'
- 'Some managers believe that office workers should be allowed to work from home as much as they want and come into the workplace only when they absolutely have to. Would this be a good idea?'

Learning to survive group exercises

Group exercises basically ask you to interact with other candidates while assessors observe your behaviour. They are looking for you to be able to contribute to a team and demonstrate some measure of social skill.

Some group exercises may ask candidates to complete a physical task such as building a tower out of children's bricks, assembling a piece of office furniture, or solving some puzzle. Other group exercises may ask you to discuss a hypothetical situation such as how to throw a great party or whether a particular organisation should proceed with a business decision or not.

Because group exercises vary enormously, you will not be able to prepare what you say. But you can think about how you behave towards others, by making sure that you:

- **Avoid dominating the discussion**. Give others an opportunity to speak and avoid interrupting them until they have finished.
- **Watch your body language**. It can be easy to drift off when other people are speaking. Always demonstrate positive body language by making eye contact with whoever is speaking, nodding, and so on.
- **Acknowledge contributions rather than criticise them**. No matter how stupid another person's point of view, try to say something that acknowledges their contribution and perhaps get someone else in the group to disagree with them on your behalf: 'That's a valid point of view. But does anyone else have a different view?'
- **Avoid jumping to conclusions**. You may have slightly different information from the other candidates. It is not uncommon for each candidate to be given one or two pieces of information that no one else has. So check whether this is the case before making any decisions.
- **Involve the quieter members of the group**. For example, if you notice that one person is particularly quiet, you could use their name and ask what they think – 'I'm not trying to pick on you, Jane, but I just want to make sure that you are happy with what's being said?'

Avoid at all costs monopolising the discussion by speaking the loudest and/or the longest.

Learning to shine in role play simulations

Role play simulations allow employers to observe how you *actually* behave, as opposed to how you *say* you would behave in a given situation. For example, you might be told that you need to step in to deal with an angry customer, a tearful colleague, or an unruly member of the team.

You will be given explicit instructions on the role play scenario. Before you start the role play scenario, be sure to:

- **Read the instructions carefully**. Note how much preparation time you have and the time you will have for the role play.
- **Make a list of questions that you want to ask**. The background materials may portray a situation that seems very black and white. You may seem right and the other person may seem to be in the wrong. However, the assessor or actor may possess information in their heads that you do not have – perhaps you are actually the one who has been deliberately misinformed by the instructions. So it always worth doing some fact-finding rather than forging ahead regardless.
- **Write down any objectives that you have**. For example, if there are five key points that you want to discuss with the assessor, you can tick these off when you actually come to the meeting.

Treat the role play scenario seriously. Of course both you and the assessor know that this is not real life. But you should treat the situation as if it were real life. Being flippant or not wanting to play along will do you no favours.

When it comes to dealing with the face-to-face role play, help yourself to perform at your best. Be sure to:

- **Build a rapport with the assessor.** The temptation on first meeting the assessor or actor might be to jump in with the main task that you have been given. But it usually makes sense to spend just a few minutes exchanging pleasantries, as you would do with any person that you are meeting for the first time.
- **Seek compromises.** Avoid charging into a role play simulation by telling the other person what you think they should do. Try to ask questions as much as tell them what you think. Seek a middle ground wherever you can.
- **Be calm and positive.** The person in the role play scenario may have instructions to try to provoke you into becoming angry, so make sure you stay calm and avoid displaying even the tiniest flash of irritation. Similarly, try to stay positive and look for positive statements you can make rather than only pointing out why the other person is wrong and needs to listen to you!

COPING WITH PANEL INTERVIEWS

Panel interviews are particularly popular in the public sector, where it is not uncommon to be faced with a row of six or seven (or even more) interviewers.

When faced with so many interviewers, you will have little chance to work on building a rapport with them. In such situations, try to:

- **Build what little rapport you can** by introducing yourself to each of the interviewers on the panel. A simple handshake and hello to each person in turn should be acceptable to even the stuffiest of panels.

- **Maintain eye contact with the person on the panel who asks you each question**. However, do also look occasionally at the other people on the panel.
- **Take your time to think before you answer each question**. With so many interviewers – each of whom has their own agenda and line of questioning – it would be easy to get confused by the interrogative nature of the panel interview.

MAKING AN IMPACT AT GROUP INTERVIEWS

Group interviews are often used to reduce a large number of candidates to a smaller number in the shortest time possible. For example, there may be a roomful of many candidates. And the interviewers may invite volunteers to stand up and introduce themselves to the interviewers and the rest of the group. Or the interviewers may pose two or three questions for each of the candidates to answer in turn.

The interviewers are looking for enthusiasm and confidence in a group situation. They are trying to eliminate candidates who clearly do not have sufficient interpersonal skills. So, make sure that you:

- Volunteer sooner rather than later. Candidates who are late to volunteer are unlikely to be taken through to further rounds of the interviewing process.
- Speak in a clear and loud enough voice for everyone to hear.
- Smile and try to appear relaxed but enthusiastic.

PERFORMING WELL DURING TELEPHONE INTERVIEWS

Increasingly, some larger organisations are using telephone

interviews to screen candidates. Telephone interviews are often much briefer than face-to-face interviews. However, you need to be just as well prepared.

In order to do well at telephone interviews, be sure to:

- Do all of your research on the company as if you were attending a face-to-face interview. You could be asked just about anything. So do your homework (see Chapter 1 of this book) on the company, think about your answers to likely questions, and prepare good questions to ask of the interviewers too.
- Prepare the workstation where you can take the call. The advantage of a telephone interview is that you can have your notes with you. So if you've worked through the questions in Chapters 4 to 8 of this book, be sure to have your notes to hand. Also make sure you have a copy of your CV at the ready too. ·
- Smile as you speak. Even though the telephone interviewer won't of course be able to see your smile, many interviewers say that they can hear when a person is smiling.
- Make an effort to inject enthusiasm into your voice. Have a glass of water at hand in case your mouth or throat gets dry. And try speaking out loud some of your interview answers immediately before the call to warm your voice up.
- Make sure you won't be disturbed. You have to make the right impact. So make sure your other telephones and electronic devices such as a pager or BlackBerry are switched off. Tell anyone you live with that you are on an important call and that they shouldn't interrupt you. If you have young children and/or animals in the house, make doubly sure that their crying/barking/whatever can't be overheard by your telephone interviewer!

SURVIVING VIDEO INTERVIEWS

In order to save time and cut costs, organisations are increasingly using webcams on computers and tablets to do video interviews. The most common piece of software used for this is Skype, although others are popular too.

To make sure that your video interview goes smoothly, ensure that you:

■ Make sure that you know how to use the video conferencing software. Ask a friend to do a practice video chat so that you are certain you know how to connect the call, control the volume of the call, adjust the picture and so on.

■ Check that you are happy with how your face is lit on camera. If the primary light source in a room is behind you, then your face may be plunged into darkness. Try positioning a lamp in front of you to make sure that the interviewer can see your facial expressions.

■ Check what the background to your video call will look like. You want to create a good impression so make sure there is an uncluttered background behind you. Showing an interviewer your drying laundry or a disorganised room may reflect badly on you.

■ Think about what you will wear for the interview. Dress in order to make a good impression. Remove any pieces of jewellery that could jangle or create distracting noises.

■ As with telephone interviews, make sure that you will not be disturbed and that background noises such as playing children or barking dogs can't be overheard.

IN SUMMARY...

■ Avoid second-guessing personality questionnaires but always answer questions giving yourself the benefit of the doubt.

■ Do a bit of practice before any aptitude test – even doing a few Sudoku puzzles or simple maths questions could help to boost your scores.

■ Keep your cool during assessment centre exercises and keep in mind the skills that the interviewers are looking for.

■ Speak up early and confidently during group interviews to make sure you get noticed.

■ Do a little preparation to help you to perform well during telephone interviews.

Chapter 11

ENDING ON A HIGH NOTE

In this chapter …
- **Making a strong final impact**
- **Writing follow-up letters**
- **Ensuring you have positive letters of reference**

By now you should have answered the interviewer's many questions and had the opportunity to ask a few of your own. You may think that there is little else you can do – but you would be wrong to think so.

LEAVING THE INTERVIEWER WITH A STRONG FINAL IMPRESSION

Experience tells us that first impressions count (in fact, the technical name for those memorable initial moments is the *primacy* effect). But psychologists have found that final impressions can also have a disproportionately large impact on how you will be remembered too (the *recency* effect).

Some points to keep in mind as you prepare to leave:

- **Check the next steps**. If it hasn't already been made clear to you, ask whether this is the only interview and when you might expect to hear about the interviewer's decision.
- **Make a final statement about your enthusiasm for the job**. 'I'd like to say that I really like what I've heard about the company. And I really look forward to being invited back for a second/third/etcetera interview.'
- **Inject enthusiasm and a positive manner into your**

departing moments. Shake hands firmly with the interviewer, smile, tell the interviewer how much you have enjoyed meeting them and learning a bit more about the organisation, and say goodbye.

Dealing with spontaneous job offers

It is unlikely that you will be offered a job on the spot. In fact, you will probably not be offered a job there and then in 95 percent of cases.

However, in those few cases where you may be in the final stage of an interview and perhaps the only remaining candidate, it can happen. If you do find yourself being offered a job at the end of an interview:

- **Express your excitement to be offered the job**. 'That's fantastic – I'm very pleased because I like what I have heard about the role and company so far.'
- **Avoid accepting the offer**. If you say yes now, you may be compromising your ability to negotiate a good package.
- **Ask for time to think about the job offer**. Avoid accepting on the spot as you may compromise your ability to ask for more money! 'I would like to accept the offer. But I want to make sure that I don't rush into a decision, so I'd like a few days to think about it.'
- **Ask for more detail about the offer in writing**. 'Would it be possible to send me a sample contract so that I can see what you are offering me?'

However, remember that it is unusual to be offered a job there and then. So do not be disappointed if the interviewer simply says goodbye.

WRITE A FOLLOW-UP LETTER IMMEDIATELY

Many candidates feel that writing a follow-up letter after an interview, like writing thank-you letters for Christmas presents, is an old-fashioned practice. However, many interviewers *are* old-fashioned in their approach and appreciate the gesture. If your letter could influence the interviewer to choose you over another candidate, surely it is worth the extra five minutes of effort?

As soon as you can, you should compose a short letter of no more than one page in length to the interviewer. I would strongly recommend that you write a physical letter rather than send an email. Your email could easily get lost amongst the hundreds of emails that most managers receive every day. So pack some writing paper, envelopes, and stamps in your interview bag. And write a letter the moment you leave the employer's premises so you can post it that same day.

The key points to get across in your letter should be that:

- **You appreciated the interview and enjoyed meeting the interviewer**. For example: 'Thank you for making the time to see me. I very much enjoyed meeting you and having the opportunity to hear about the aggressive growth plans that the business has.'
- **That you are enthusiastic about the job, the people, the challenge, or the company**. For example: 'The more I think about it, the more I believe that your plans for growth will make the business a very exciting place to be in over the next few years.'
- **That you have the right skills and experience for the vacancy**. Go on to recap in only one or two paragraphs what you believe those key skills and experiences are. For example:

'I feel that my track record would make me an asset to your team. In particular, I have proven that I can deliver revenue growth quickly in the pharmaceuticals sector. Furthermore, I am sure that my work alongside external suppliers to implement change initiatives would also be of value.'

■ **That you would very much like the job (or to be invited back for the next round of interview)**. 'As such, I would very much like to be a part of the company. I realise that there is another round of interviews with the main board, and I would welcome the opportunity to convince them that I am the person for the job.'

Given that you've invested hours in researching a job and turning up for an interview, be sure to take five minutes to write a follow-up letter.

MAKING SURE YOUR LETTERS OF REFERENCE WILL BE POSITIVE

Most job offers are made 'subject to satisfactory references'. If you've been offered a job, it would be a shame for your references to let you down. Amazingly enough, some candidates ask former bosses and colleagues to write references for them without ensuring that those references will give them the best chance of getting the job as possible.

To ensure that your references will be suitably glowing, always speak to your referees – either in person or over the telephone – to ask whether they would be happy to give you an unreservedly positive reference. If your referee sounds at all reluctant or hesitant to be unremittingly positive about you, you must understand their concerns! If a referee is unwilling to be relentlessly positive about you, you may even need to decide to find a different referee.

Once you have chosen a referee, it also makes sense to remind them of the key skills, experiences and qualities that you would like them to emphasise when writing about you.

A sample letter to a referee

Dear Judy,

Thank you for agreeing to write a reference for me. As I explained on the telephone, I am applying to market research companies for a job as a researcher.

It would help me greatly if you could emphasise certain experiences from when I worked in your team:

- Account-managing major clients such as Maximus Dog Foods and Parnassus TV Productions.
- Running focus groups and using quantitative surveys to evaluate brand impact of our clients' consumer goods.
- Presenting results to clients.

I will telephone you in the next few days to see whether I can answer any other questions that you may have.

Best wishes,
Simon

If possible, ask your referees if they would mind giving you a draft of what they intend to write about you. If you are asked by an interviewer to provide references, you can be confident of exactly what they will say about you.

IN SUMMARY...

- Use the 'recency effect' work to your advantage by making a final statement about your enthusiasm for the job, and focusing on projecting your positive attitude through your body language and a simple smile right before you leave.
- Avoid accepting job offers on the spot as you could compromise your ability to negotiate the best package.
- Write a follow-up letter the moment you leave the interview to demonstrate to the interviewer your enthusiasm for the job.
- Brief your referees on what you would like them to say about you to potential employers to ensure that you don't get stung by any nasty surprises.

Chapter 12

SIGNING ON THE DOTTED LINE

In this chapter …
- **Reviewing your performance and asking for feedback**
- **Negotiating the best possible salary and benefits package**
- **Making sure a job really is right for you**

With sufficient preparation and practice, you may find yourself getting more than one offer! But even the best candidates get knocked back occasionally – so it's worth reviewing your own performance and asking for feedback on what you could have done differently.

Eventually though, you will get an offer. And the next-to-last step before joining any employer is to tackle the not-so-small matter of agreeing how much you should get paid. And, before you accept the offer, are you really, really, really sure it's the right move for you?

HANDLING REJECTION AND LEARNING FROM YOUR EXPERIENCES

Even the best candidates get knocked back occasionally. You may feel disappointed, angry or resentful not to get a job. But there can be all sorts of reasons for you not to get the offer. Perhaps you didn't do anything wrong but there was simply a favoured internal candidate in the running who was pretty much always going to get the job. On the other hand, be careful not to get blasé – perhaps you *could* have performed better.

Don't let rejection get you down. Take an evening off and do something that you really enjoy. Forget about the job hunt for a while and let your hair down. Come back to the interview process fresher. So long as you learn from each interview that you go to, you will get better and eventually get the job that is right for you.

Analysing your own performance

If you didn't get offered the job, it's a good idea to think about how well the interview went. Firstly, take a few minutes to ask yourself the following questions:

- **What went well?** What were you pleased with?
- **What went badly?** What would you do differently if you could do that interview all over again? Were you asked any questions that you did not have a good answer for?
- **What would you do differently?** What have you learned that you could apply to future interviews?

Don't move on until you have jotted down some thoughts to each of these questions.

Next, think about the following criteria to evaluate specific aspects of your interview performance. Rate your interview performance out of ten for each one of the criteria (1 = 'terrible and could do much, much better', 5 = 'average and could still do better', and 10 = 'perfect and did not for one moment go wrong'):

- **Research**. How would you rate your fact-finding and knowledge about the company? Did you know everything about the company, their industry, competitors, their strategy and structure? Did you also research the format of the interview and know exactly how many interviews and interviewers there would be at each stage?

- **Questions and answers**. How well did you respond to each of the questions that you were asked? Did you have good examples to show off your key qualities and skills? Were there any questions that you could have answered better?
- **Rapport with the interviewer**. Did you engage in polite conversation and put the interviewer at ease? Did you maintain a good posture throughout the interview? Did you use your tone of voice and body language to make the interviewer comfortable?
- **My questions**. Did you ask sensible questions? Did those questions show that you were not only knowledgeable but also enthusiastic and motivated?
- **Follow-up letter**. Did your letter make good points about your skills and experience without tipping over the edge and becoming corny? You could even show a copy of the letter to your friends and ask them to comment on it.

Now go back through your scores. For any area that you scored less than 8 out of 10, think about what you could have done better.

Gathering feedback on your interview performance

The most valuable source of information about your interview performance comes directly from the interviewer. As soon as you have confirmation that you have been rejected, you should give the interviewer a call.

Explain to the interviewer that feedback would be invaluable, as you would like to know what you could have done better. Be polite but persistent. Some questions to ask could include:

- 'Did you have any concerns about my experience or CV?'

- 'Were there any questions that you felt I didn't answer to your satisfaction?'
- 'Do you have any suggestions as to what I could have done to make a better impression on you?'
- 'Would you be able to tell me what the successful candidate did or said that helped him or her get the job over me?'

Many interviewers are loath to give negative feedback, so you will almost certainly have to ring the interviewer several times. Persist – but do it politely! When you do manage to speak to the interviewer, encourage them to be completely candid in giving you feedback. Emphasise again the fact that the feedback would help you to prepare more effectively for future interviews.

Use a conversation with an interviewer to hone your performance in your next interview rather than to argue over their impression of you. At this stage, it is highly unlikely that you will be able to change the interviewer's mind. The interviewer has done you the favour of providing you with some honest feedback. So the least you can do is listen to it with good grace.

Only when you are off the telephone should you think about the feedback:

- Were there any pleasant surprises in the feedback?
- Were there any unpleasant shocks in the feedback? And what should you therefore do differently in a future interview?

If you find yourself being invited to more than a handful of interviews but that you aren't getting any offers, think about setting up a mock interview (see Chapter 3) with a friend to get some candid feedback on what you may be doing wrong.

NEGOTIATING THE BEST POSSIBLE SALARY AND PACKAGE

It's a great feeling to be offered a job, but resist the temptation to accept the offer immediately. Right now, the employer wants you *but does not have you*, which puts you in a privileged position. Now is the best time to try to negotiate a good salary and pay package. It is far more difficult to achieve pay rises and bonuses when you are working for an employer. Job changes provide most people with the best opportunity they will ever have to achieve a better deal at work. So ask now, or regret it later.

Set up a face-to-face meeting with the employer. Explain that you are pleased to have been made the offer, but that you have a few more questions to ask about the company before deciding whether to accept or not. The following steps may help you to negotiate:

1. Estimate your worth

If you have been working for one employer for a number of years, your pay may be out of line with the going market rate. So check beforehand what someone of your experience could be making in other companies. To establish a realistic salary range, you should:

- Read job advertisements in the press.
- Talk to recruitment consultants and agencies who specialise in placing people with your skills and experience.
- Look at salary surveys on recruitment websites.
- Ask friends and colleagues in similar lines of work for their opinions.

But do not get too fixated on the salary. There are many other elements of a remuneration package that you should think about, such as:

- Pension contributions, medical benefits, life insurance, and other benefits.
- Season ticket loan, car allowance or company car.
- Bonuses, share options, or profit share.
- Gym membership and expense accounts.
- Payment of course tuition fees or time off to study for external exams.
- Mobile phone and laptop computer.
- Flexible working – such as the number of hours or days that you work a week, or the freedom to work from home on certain days.

2. Figure out your wants and needs

Negotiation is a process of trading off some of your superficial wants to achieve what you need. So prepare by thinking through the following questions:

- **What do you *want*?** In an ideal world, what would you like the employer to offer you?
- **What do you *need*?** In a more realistic world, what is the minimum that you are willing to accept from the employer? If the employer's offer is too low, you should have a lower limit in mind at which you will decline the job.
- **What benefits can you deliver to the employer?** Why should the employer give you what you want? What are your arguments going to be? What can you do for the employer to justify an increased pay package?
- **What minor concessions are you willing to make?** What would you be willing to give up or trade off to ensure that you get what you need? For example, you might be willing to put up with a smaller base salary for a bigger pension contribution and bonus.

3. Prepare to negotiate courteously

You have little to lose if you ask for a better deal. However, there is a big difference between asking and demanding. Asking politely and listening to the employer's responses and reaching a compromise is acceptable to most employers, while demanding more in an aggressive manner could lead the employer to retract the job offer entirely. Giving ultimatums could appear adversarial and turn the employer off.

4. Wait for the employer to mention money

When you meet the employer, use the meeting as an opportunity to find out more about them. Ask questions to check whether this is a company that you would like to work for – for example, you might use this opportunity to ask further questions from Chapter 9.

The employer will eventually broach the subject, perhaps by asking you how much it would take to get you. If you possibly can, try to get the employer to mention a figure first. Negotiating a pay package is like playing poker – whoever reveals their hand first is in the weaker position.

If the figure is too low for your liking, try to express your desire for more by selling the benefits that the employer would gain by employing you – for example: 'I would have thought that with my IT skills, I'd be worth more than that.' And then put the pressure back on the employer with a question: 'Do you think that's reasonable?'

But don't forget to offer up some concessions while negotiating too.

In your negotiations, avoid being the first to mention money – if you mention money too early on, the employer will think that you are motivated by money and little else.

5. Get it in writing

Once you and the employer have reached an agreement, ask for a letter to confirm the details in writing. It does not have to be a formal contract – just a letter outlining all of your terms of employment. Receiving an offer in writing avoids mistakes or misunderstandings later.

CHECKING THAT A JOB REALLY IS RIGHT FOR YOU

Looking for a new job is a stressful process. But just because you have a financially beneficial offer on the table may not mean that you will be happy. More pay could just mean longer hours, more travel, or a tougher working environment.

Before you accept that job offer, consider the following questions carefully:

- Do you like the work itself? Would you find the job sufficiently challenging or interesting?
- Are you happy with your prospective boss? Have you met and talked about the sort of targets that you would have to achieve? Does your boss strike you as the sort of person that you would get on with? If you felt uncomfortable being interviewed for only an hour by your prospective boss, how would you feel about working together for several years?
- Do you like your prospective colleagues? Would you be able to work and socialise with them?

- Do you understand the politics of the organisation? And are you comfortable with the company's culture?
- Do you understand your future prospects in the company?

If your honest answers to those questions are 'yes', then this really is the job for you. Write back to the employer to accept that job, go celebrate, and let me know how you get on (rob@talentspace.co.uk). Well done!

IN SUMMARY…

- Recognise that you will not get every job you interview for. Don't let it get you down but do reflect on your performance. Go through each of the questions and consider whether your response was as good as it could possibly have been.
- Persist in chasing the interviewer until you get some post-interview feedback. Reassure the interviewer that you will not get defensive or try to change their mind. But make sure that you take their feedback on board.
- Estimate your worth and be prepared to prove why you are worth more before asking for a better package.
- Think about the job. Just because you have an offer does not mean that you must take it. Will the job fulfil both your personal and professional needs?

Chapter 13

BUILDING RAPPORT AND PROJECTING CONFIDENCE

In this chapter ...
- **Learning to use body language to build rapport**
- **Building rapport by behaving positively**
- **Using body language to pump up your confidence**
- **Turning nervousness into excitement**

You've probably heard the saying that it's *not* what *you say but* how *you say it, that counts*. In most of the chapters in this book, we have been focusing on making sure that you have smart answers to even the toughest questions that interviewers might ask you. But in this final chapter, we will cover some advanced techniques to ensure that you make a great impression and leave a positive, lasting impact on the interviewer.

We already covered some of the basics of making an impact in Chapters 2 and 3. Before we move on, you might like to make sure that you have mastered the advice in those chapters first. Learn to walk before you try to run!

USING BODY LANGUAGE TO BUILD RAPPORT

I mentioned in Chapter 1 that interviewers are looking for candidates who can fulfil the so-called 'four Cs' of interview performance: competence, commitment, confidence, chemistry. Let's begin this chapter by looking at how you can create chemistry.

Psychological research tells us that we can build rapport simply by copying other people's body language. Even better, studies tell us that people don't generally realise when they are being copied – they simply feel a greater liking for the person who is copying them!

The following technique goes by many names. Some people call it 'mirroring' while others call it 'mimicking'. But regardless of what it's called, the idea is simply to copy *some* of the *broad* body movements that an interviewer makes. In order to build rapport, make an effort to:

- Mimic some of the interviewer's mannerisms. For example, if the interviewer leans backwards in her chair, then you should wait a couple of seconds and then lean back in your chair too. If the interviewer sits forwards and puts an elbow on the table, then again wait a few seconds and then do the same too.
- Make sure that your mimicry is subtle! Only mimic some of the interviewer's gestures as opposed to every move. If you copy an interviewer's movements too carefully or too quickly (i.e. without a pause each time), then it is more likely that the interviewer will catch on.
- Vary the length of time between an interviewer's movements and your mimicry. Sometimes it may be fine to copy a gesture or bodily movement very quickly – within a second or two. But at other times you should aim to copy the gesture much more slowly – perhaps after five to ten seconds.

Many studies show that mimicry helps to build rapport and create chemistry. However, make sure that you don't put so much effort into your mimicry that you lose focus on the questions you're being asked or the answers you are giving. Mimicry should be something that you do *in addition* to listening carefully to questions and giving robust answers

– it's not something you do *instead* of answering interview questions well!

DEMONSTRATING YOUR ENTHUSIASM AND PASSION

Succeeding at job interviews is not only about giving well-crafted answers to all of the questions that you arc asked. Employers don't just want to hire competent employees; they also want to hire committed individuals who genuinely seem to want the job.

In order to convince an interviewer that you really, *really* want the job, it's worth finding at least a couple of occasions during an interview to flatter the organisation and express your enthusiasm for the role.

Begin by preparing at least two or three positive statements that you can make about the company. You may not be able to mention all of these statements, but by researching the organisation and preparing at least a few different things to say, you will have a better chance of being able to mention one or two of them than if you don't prepare. Some examples:

■ 'I really like the idea of working for a large, successful firm like yours because of the opportunities to move around from store to store.'
■ 'Of course I want to work for a small, family-owned business because I think that people look after each other better within smaller companies.'

As you can see from those two examples, they are ways to flatter an interviewer about an organisation despite those organisations being the complete opposite of each other. So what could *you* praise your next interviewer's organisation about?

A related idea is to ensure that you mention at least once how much you want the job. A good opportunity to make this kind of positive statement is when an interviewer asks if you have any questions. After asking whatever questions you may have, you could finish by saying something like:

- 'I just want to say that I really do want this job. I am interviewing with a couple of companies but I really like the product range that you offer and I think that I would get a real buzz out of working here and selling those products.'
- 'No more questions, but I'd like to finish by saying that I've really enjoyed this interview. I've had the opportunity to learn more about the actual work and the culture of the company and I'm definitely more certain that I want to work for the company now than I was before the interview.'

Remember that answering interview questions well is only part of the equation for being offered the job. Show an interviewer that you are committed to the industry and this particular organisation and you may just get the offer you want.

USING BODY LANGUAGE TO BOOST YOUR CONFIDENCE

We already discussed some basic techniques in Chapter 3 for handling nerves and feeling calmer and more confident. However, the very latest research points to a new method of feeling more confident and performing well during interviews.

Columbia University researchers Dana Carney and Andy Yap, along with their Harvard University collaborator Amy Cuddy, have demonstrated in a series of experiments that our physical postures can change our hormonal levels, which then alter how we feel about ourselves. Effectively, how we hold ourselves can either reduce or boost our confidence.

For example, when people sit with slumped shoulders and their hands in their laps, this reduces levels of hormones such as testosterone which makes them feel less powerful and less confident. Or when people either stand or sit with hands crossed across their chests and knees crossed, this again makes them feel less confident.

However, when people stand with their chests thrust forward and their hands on their hips, they experience higher levels of testosterone, which tends to make them feel more powerful and confident. Similarly, when people sit with their legs extended and their feet up on a table, this posture helps them to feel more powerful and confident.

I'm not suggesting that you put your feet up on a table during an interview. However, you can use this technique in the minutes *before* an interview to give yourself a mental boost.

If you are seated, for example, in a waiting area before an interview:

- Make sure that you sit with an expansive body posture. That means extending your elbows away from your body, for example, either by putting your hands on your hips or perhaps locking your hands behind your head.
- If you're a man, try to sit in an expansive position with your knees apart too. If you're a woman, be careful if you are wearing a skirt!

Alternatively, find somewhere you can't be observed (e.g. an empty toilet cubicle) and adopt an expansive posture for 60 seconds. Ideally, stand with your hands on your hips with your feet wider than your shoulders.

If you like, you could combine this physical exercise with one of the psychological techniques from Chapter 3 or the reappraisal technique we're going to cover next in this chapter. This so-called power posture technique may sound a little unorthodox, but trust the science underpinning it.

HANDLING NERVES BY HARNESSING YOUR EXCITEMENT

This next technique is called reappraisal. It involves thinking about the situation you're facing in a different way. So rather than seeing an interview as something that is scary and threatening, we can train ourselves to see it as something that is exciting and as an opportunity.

But allow me to explain a little about how our emotions work first. We experience fear because the emotion helps to mobilise our bodies to function in times of danger. Fear triggers circuits in the brain that cause various hormonal releases. For example, we experience a surge of adrenaline which makes our hearts beat faster. We breathe more quickly too. All of this is part of the so-called 'fight or flight' response, which is designed to help us to either fight off a predator or flee danger.

The fight-or-flight response was a perfectly sensible way of behaving for our ancestors who had to deal with lots of genuinely life-endangering circumstances. Our ancient predecessors had to fight off animals as well as other people. They were literally in danger of losing life or limb.

But modern situations don't usually present any real danger to us. Yes, interviews may *feel* scary, but we're unlikely to face any actual physical danger!

The next time you are sitting and waiting to be interviewed then, remember:

- Take a realistic perspective on an interview. Please realise that an interview does not present an actual physical threat to you.
- Remember that you will not be in danger of being physically attacked. Regardless of what you do or say during the interview, bear in mind that there are no negative physical consequences that you have to be concerned with.
- Instead, tell yourself, 'I'm excited!' Think about the possible positive things that could come out of the interview. Tell yourself, 'I'm excited!' at least a few times and you help to persuade your own mind to feel differently.

IN SUMMARY...
- Mimic the broad gestures and bodily postures of an interviewer in order to build rapport.
- Find at least a handful of opportunities during an interview to either flatter the organisation by saying something positive about it or expressing your enthusiasm for the work.
- Adopt a powerful, expansive posture for 60 seconds before an interview in order to buoy your confidence.
- Remember that interviews may be scary but you are not actually in any physical danger. Tell yourself that you are excited instead.

APPENDIX

ANSWERS TO PRACTICE PSYCHOMETRIC TEST QUESTIONS

Here are the answers to the psychometric tests from Chapter 10.

Psychometric Test 1

1. 1,230 units
2. £224
3. £209
4. 10.45am
5. 26 minutes
6. £68
7. 5/8
8. 25,080 times
9. £315.25
10. £35

Psychometric Test 2

1. C
2. D
3. C
4. A
5. B
6. A
7. D
8. C
9. B
10. D

INDEX OF QUESTIONS

INDEX OF QUESTIONS BY TOPIC

INDEX